Microsoft® PowerPoint® 2010

ILLUSTRATED

Brief

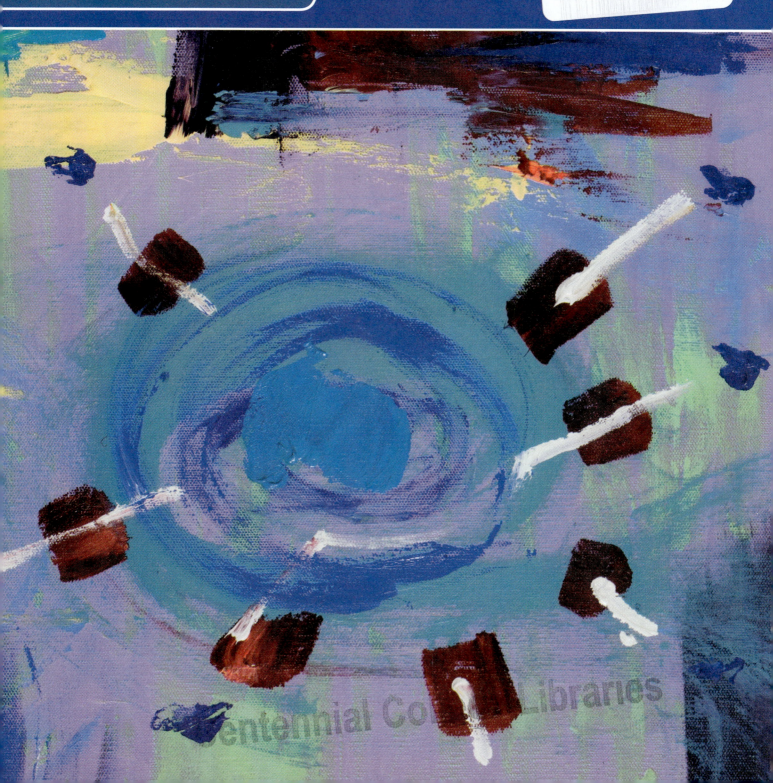

Microsoft® PowerPoint® 2010

ILLUSTRATED

Brief

David W. Beskeen

COURSE TECHNOLOGY
CENGAGE Learning·

Australia · Brazil · Japan · Korea · Mexico · Singapore · Spain · United Kingdom · United States

COURSE TECHNOLOGY
CENGAGE Learning

Microsoft® PowerPoint® 2010—Illustrated Brief
David W. Beskeen

Vice President, Publisher: Nicole Jones Pinard

Executive Editor: Marjorie Hunt

Associate Acquisitions Editor: Brandi Shailer

Senior Product Manager: Christina Kling Garrett

Associate Product Manager: Michelle Camisa

Editorial Assistant: Kim Klasner

Director of Marketing: Cheryl Costantini

Senior Marketing Manager: Ryan DeGrote

Marketing Coordinator: Kristen Panciocco

Contributing Authors: Carol Cram, Elizabeth Eisner Reding

Developmental Editors: Rachel Biheller Bunin, Pamela Conrad, Jeanne Herring

Content Project Manager: Lisa Weidenfeld

Copy Editor: Mark Goodin

Proofreader: Harry Johnson

Indexer: BIM Indexing and Proofreading Services

QA Manuscript Reviewers: John Frietas, Serge Palladino, Jeff Schwartz, Danielle Shaw, Marianne Snow

Print Buyer: Fola Orekoya

Cover Designer: GEX Publishing Services

Cover Artist: Mark Hunt

Composition: GEX Publishing Services

Credits:
Figure Credit line
C-5 Photo courtesy of Janet Moffat
C-18 Photo courtesy of Jennifer Beskeen
C-21, C-22 Photos courtesy of Barbara Clemens
D-3 Photo courtesy of Donna Goudy
D-4, D-5 Photos courtesy of Janet Moffat

For product information and technology assistance, contact us at
Cengage Learning Customer & Sales Support, 1-800-354-9706
For permission to use material from this text or product, submit all requests online at **www.cengage.com/permissions**
Further permissions questions can be emailed to
permissionrequest@cengage.com

Trademarks:

Some of the product names and company names used in this book have been used for identification purposes only and may be trademarks or registered trademarks of their respective manufacturers and sellers.

Microsoft and the Office logo are either registered trademarks or trademarks of Microsoft Corporation in the United States and/or other countries. Course Technology, Cengage Learning is an independent entity from Microsoft Corporation, and not affiliated with Microsoft in any manner.

Library of Congress Control Number: 2010930078

ISBN-13: 978-0-538-74830-8
ISBN-10: 0-538-74830-3

Course Technology
20 Channel Center Street
Boston, MA 02210
USA

Cengage Learning is a leading provider of customized learning solutions with office locations around the globe, including Singapore, the United Kingdom, Australia, Mexico, Brazil, and Japan. Locate your local office at:
www.cengage.com/global

Cengage Learning products are represented in Canada by Nelson Education, Ltd.

To learn more about Course Technology, visit **www.cengage.com/coursetechnology**

To learn more about Cengage Learning, visit **www.cengage.com**

Purchase any of our products at your local college store or at our preferred online store **www.cengagebrain.com**

Printed in the United States of America
2 3 4 5 6 7 8 9 18 17 16 15 14 13 12 11

Brief Contents

Contents

Web Apps

Preface

Welcome to *Microsoft PowerPoint 2010— Illustrated Brief*. If this is your first experience with the Illustrated series, you'll see that this book has a unique design: each skill is presented on two facing pages, with steps on the left and screens on the right. The layout makes it easy to learn a skill without having to read a lot of text and flip pages to see an illustration.

This book is an ideal learning tool for a wide range of learners—the "rookies" will find the clean design easy to follow and focused with only essential information presented, and the "hotshots" will appreciate being able to move quickly through the lessons to find the information they need without reading a lot of text. The design also makes this a great reference after the course is over! See the illustration on the right to learn more about the pedagogical and design elements of a typical lesson.

What's New In This Edition

- **Fully Updated.** Highlights the new features of Microsoft PowerPoint 2010 including new 3-D motion slide transitions, artistic effects and textures for pictures, organizing slides into sections, turning your mouse into a laser pointer, and the new Backstage view. New Appendix covers cloud computing concepts and using Microsoft Office Web Apps. Examples and exercises are updated throughout.

- **Maps to SAM 2010.** This book is designed to work with SAM (Skills Assessment Manager) 2010. **SAM Assessment** contains performance-based, hands-on SAM exams for each unit of this book, and **SAM Training** provides hands-on training for skills covered in the book. Each Independent Challenge 1 exercise is available in **SAM Projects**, which is auto-grading software that provides both students and instructors with immediate, detailed feedback (SAM sold separately.) See page xii for more information on SAM.

Each two-page spread focuses on a single skill.

Introduction briefly explains why the lesson skill is important.

A case scenario motivates the the steps and puts learning in context.

UNIT B
PowerPoint 2010

Using Proofing and Language Tools

As your work on the presentation file nears completion, you need to review and proofread your slides thoroughly for errors. You can use the spell-checking feature in PowerPoint to check for and correct spelling errors. This feature compares the spelling of all the words in your presentation against the words contained in PowerPoint's electronic dictionary. You still must proofread your presentation for punctuation, grammar, and word-usage errors because the spell checker recognizes only misspelled and unknown words, not misused words. For example, the spell checker would not identify the word "last" as an error, even if you had intended to type the word "cast." PowerPoint also includes language tools that translate words or phrases from your default language into another language using the Microsoft Translator. You're finished working on the presentation for now, so it's a good time to check spelling. You then experiment with language translation because the final presentation will be translated into French.

STEPS

TROUBLE
If your spell checker finds another word, such as your name on Slide 1, click Ignore All in the spelling dialog box.

1. Click the **Review tab** on the Ribbon, then click the **Spelling button** in the Proofing group
   PowerPoint begins to check the spelling in your presentation. When PowerPoint finds a misspelled word or a word it doesn't recognize, the Spelling dialog box opens, as shown in Figure B-15. In this case, PowerPoint identifies the misspelled word on Slide 4 and suggests you replace it with the correctly spelled word "Exclusive."

2. Click **Change**
   PowerPoint changes the misspelled word and then continues to check the rest of the presentation for errors. If PowerPoint finds any other words it does not recognize, either change or ignore them. When the spell checker finishes checking your presentation, the Spelling dialog box closes, and an alert box opens with a message that the spelling check is complete.

QUICK TIP
The spell checker does not check the text in inserted pictures or objects.

3. Click **OK**, click the **Slide 1 thumbnail** in the Slides tab, then save your presentation
   The alert box closes. Now you need to see how the language translation feature works.

4. Click the **Translate button** in the Language group, then click **Choose Translation Language**
   The Translation Language Options dialog box opens.

5. Click the **Translate to list arrow**, click **French (France)**, then click **OK**
   The Translation Language Options dialog box closes.

6. Click the **Translate button** in the Language group, click **Mini Translator [French(France)]**, click anywhere in the footer text object, then select all of the text
   The Microsoft Translator begins to analyze the selected text and a semitransparent Microsoft Translator box appears below the text.

QUICK TIP
To copy the translated text to a slide, click the Copy button at the bottom of the Microsoft Translator box, right-click the slide, then click a Paste option.

7. Move the pointer over the **Microsoft Translator box**
   A French translation of the text appears as shown in Figure B-16. The translation language setting remains in effect until you reset it.

8. Click the **Translate button** in the Language group, click **Choose Translation Language**, click the **Translate to list arrow**, click **Arabic**, click **OK**, click the **Translate button again**, then click **Mini Translator [Arabic]**
   The Mini Translator is turned off and the translation language is restored to the default setting.

9. Submit your presentation to your instructor, then exit PowerPoint

PowerPoint 40 Modifying a Presentation

Tips and troubleshooting advice, right where you need it—next to the step itself.

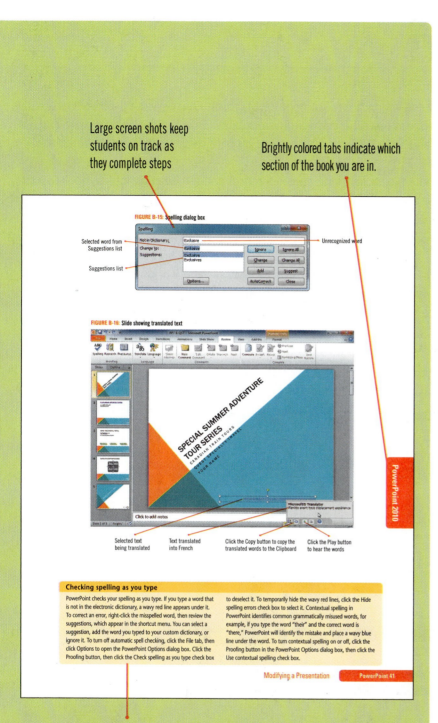

Large screen shots keep students on track as they complete steps

Brightly colored tabs indicate which section of the book you are in.

Clues to Use boxes provide useful information related to the lesson skill.

Assignments

The lessons use Quest Specialty Travel, a fictional adventure travel company, as the case study. The assignments on the light yellow pages at the end of each unit increase in difficulty. Assignments include:

- **Concepts Review** consist of multiple choice, matching, and screen identification questions.

- **Skills Reviews** are hands-on, step-by-step exercises that review the skills covered in each lesson in the unit.

- **Independent Challenges** are case projects requiring critical thinking and application of the unit skills. The Independent Challenges increase in difficulty, with the first one in each unit being the easiest. Independent Challenges 2 and 3 become increasingly open-ended, requiring more independent problem solving.

- **SAM Projects** is live-in-the-application autograding software that provides immediate and detailed feedback reports to students and instructors. Each Independent Challenge 1 exercise in this book is available in SAM Projects. (Purchase of a SAM Projects pincode is required).

- **Real Life Independent Challenges** are practical exercises in which students create documents to help them with their every day lives.

- **Advanced Challenge Exercises** set within the Independent Challenges provide optional steps for more advanced students.

- **Visual Workshops** are practical, self-graded capstone projects that require independent problem solving.

About SAM

SAM is the premier proficiency-based assessment and training environment for Microsoft Office. Web-based software along with an inviting user interface provide maximum teaching and learning flexibility. SAM builds students' skills and confidence with a variety of real-life simulations, and SAM Projects' assignments prepare students for today's workplace.

The SAM system includes Assessment, Training, and Projects, featuring page references and remediation for this book as well as Course Technology's Microsoft Office textbooks. With SAM, instructors can enjoy the flexibility of creating assignments based on content from their favorite Microsoft Office books or based on specific course objectives. Instructors appreciate the scheduling and reporting options that have made SAM the market-leading online testing and training software for over a decade. Over 2,000 performance-based questions and matching Training simulations, as well as tens of thousands of objective-based questions from many Course Technology texts, provide instructors with a variety of choices across multiple applications from the introductory level through the comprehensive level. The inclusion of hands-on Projects guarantee that student knowledge will skyrocket from the practice of solving real-world situations using Microsoft Office software.

SAM Assessment

- Content for these hands-on, performance-based tasks includes Word, Excel, Access, PowerPoint, Internet Explorer, Outlook, and Windows. Includes tens of thousands of objective-based questions from many Course Technology texts.

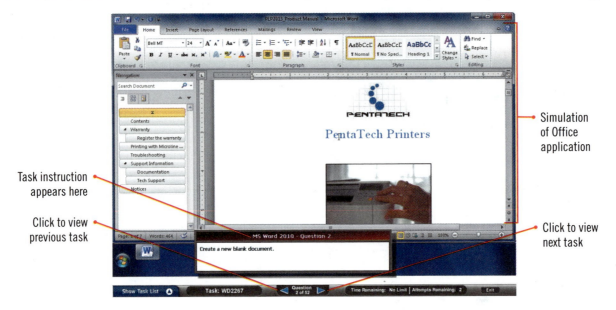

SAM Training

- Observe mode allows the student to watch and listen to a task as it is being completed.
- Practice mode allows the student to follow guided arrows and hear audio prompts to help visual learners know how to complete a task.
- Apply mode allows the student to prove what they've learned by completing a task using helpful instructions.

SAM Projects

- Live-in-the-application assignments in Word, Excel, Access and PowerPoint that help students be sure they know how to effectively communicate, solve a problem or make a decision.
- Students receive detailed feedback on their project within minutes.
- Additionally, teaches proper file management techniques.
- Ensures that academic integrity is not compromised, with unique anti-cheating detection encrypted into the data files.

Instructor Resources

The Instructor Resources CD is Course Technology's way of putting the resources and information needed to teach and learn effectively into your hands. With an integrated array of teaching and learning tools that offer you and your students a broad range of technology-based instructional options, we believe this CD represents the highest quality and most cutting edge resources available to instructors today. The resources available with this book are:

- **Instructor's Manual**—Available as an electronic file, the Instructor's Manual includes detailed lecture topics with teaching tips for each unit.

- **Sample Syllabus**—Prepare and customize your course easily using this sample course outline.

- **PowerPoint Presentations**—Each unit has a corresponding PowerPoint presentation that you can use in lecture, distribute to your students, or customize to suit your course.

- **Figure Files**—The figures in the text are provided on the Instructor Resources CD to help you illustrate key topics or concepts. You can create traditional overhead transparencies by printing the figure files. Or you can create electronic slide shows by using the figures in a presentation program such as PowerPoint.

- **Solutions to Exercises**—Solutions to Exercises contains every file students are asked to create or modify in the lessons and end-of-unit material. Also provided in this section, there is a document outlining the solutions for the end-of-unit Concepts Review, Skills Review, and Independent Challenges. An Annotated Solution File and Grading Rubric accompany each file and can be used together for quick and easy grading.

- **Data Files for Students**—To complete most of the units in this book, your students will need Data Files. You can post the Data Files on a file server for students to copy. The Data Files are available on the Instructor Resources CD-ROM, the Review Pack, and can also be downloaded from cengagebrain.com. For information on how to download the Data Files from cengagebrain.com, see the inside back cover.

Instruct students to use the Data Files List included on the Review Pack and the Instructor Resources CD. This list gives instructions on copying and organizing files.

- **ExamView**—ExamView is a powerful testing software package that allows you to create and administer printed, computer (LAN-based), and Internet exams. ExamView includes hundreds of questions that correspond to the topics covered in this text, enabling students to generate detailed study guides that include page references for further review. The computer-based and Internet testing components allow students to take exams at their computers, and also saves you time by grading each exam automatically.

Content for Online Learning.

Course Technology has partnered with the leading distance learning solution providers and class-management platforms today. To access this material, visit www.cengage.com/webtutor and search for your title. Instructor resources include the following: additional case projects, sample syllabi, PowerPoint presentations, and more. For additional information, please contact your sales representative. For students to access this material, they must have purchased a WebTutor PIN-code specific to this title and your campus platform. The resources for students might include (based on instructor preferences): topic reviews, review questions, practice tests, and more.

Acknowledgements

Instructor Advisory Board

We thank our Instructor Advisory Board who gave us their opinions and guided our decisions as we developed this new edition. They are as follows:

Terri Helfand, Chaffey Community College

Barbara Comfort, J. Sargeant Reynolds Community College

Brenda Nielsen, Mesa Community College

Sharon Cotman, Thomas Nelson Community College

Marian Meyer, Central New Mexico Community College

Audrey Styer, Morton College

Richard Alexander, Heald College

Xiaodong Qiao, Heald College

Student Advisory Board

We also thank our Student Advisory Board members, who shared their experiences using the book and offered suggestions to make it better: **Latasha Jefferson**, Thomas Nelson Community College, **Gary Williams**, Thomas Nelson Community College, **Stephanie Miller**, J. Sargeant Reynolds Community College, **Sarah Styer**, Morton Community College, **Missy Marino**, Chaffey College

Author Acknowledgements

David W. Beskeen Being a part of the extremely talented and experienced Office Illustrated team makes working on this book that much more enjoyable—many thanks to Rachel Biheller Bunin, Christina Kling Garrett, the production group, the testers, and the rest of the Cengage team! I also want to acknowledge my family, especially my parents Don and Darlene, for all they have done for me...I am forever grateful.

Dedication

This book is dedicated to the memory of Donald W. Beskeen.

Read This Before You Begin

What are Data Files?

A Data File is a partially completed PowerPoint presentation or another type of file that you use to complete the steps in the units and exercises to create the final document that you submit to your instructor. Each unit opener page lists the Data Files that you need for that unit.

Where are the Data Files?

Your instructor will provide the Data Files to you or direct you to a location on a network drive from which you can download them. For information on how to download the Data Files from cengagebrain.com, see the inside back cover.

What software was used to write and test this book?

This book was written and tested using a typical installation of Microsoft Office 2010 Professional Plus on a computer with a typical installation of Microsoft Windows 7 Ultimate.

The browser used for any Web-dependent steps is Internet Explorer 8.

Do I need to be connected to the Internet to complete the steps and exercises in this book?

Some of the exercises in this book require that your computer be connected to the Internet. If you are not connected to the Internet, see your instructor for information on how to complete the exercises.

What do I do if my screen is different from the figures shown in this book?

This book was written and tested on computers with monitors set at a resolution of 1024 × 768. If your screen shows more or less information than the figures in the book, your monitor is probably set at a higher or lower resolution. If you don't see something on your screen, you might have to scroll down or up to see the object identified in the figures.

The Ribbon—the blue area at the top of the screen—in Microsoft Office 2010 adapts to different resolutions. If your monitor is set at a lower resolution than 1024 × 768, you might not see all of the buttons shown in the figures. The groups of buttons will always appear, but the entire group might be condensed into a single button that you need to click to access the buttons described in the instructions.

COURSECASTS Learning on the Go. Always Available…Always Relevant.

Our fast-paced world is driven by technology. You know because you are an active participant—always on the go, always keeping up with technological trends, and always learning new ways to embrace technology to power your life. Let CourseCasts, hosted by Ken Baldauf of Florida State University, be your guide into weekly updates in this ever-changing space. These timely, relevant podcasts are produced weekly and are available for download at http://coursecasts.course.com or directly from iTunes (search by CourseCasts). CourseCasts are a perfect solution to getting students (and even instructors) to learn on the go!

Getting Started with Microsoft Office 2010

Files You Will Need:

OFFICE A-1.xlsx

Microsoft Office 2010 is a group of software programs designed to help you create documents, collaborate with coworkers, and track and analyze information. Each program is designed so you can work quickly and efficiently to create professional-looking results. You use different Office programs to accomplish specific tasks, such as writing a letter or producing a sales presentation, yet all the programs have a similar look and feel. Once you become familiar with one program, you'll find it easy to transfer your knowledge to the others. This unit introduces you to the most frequently used programs in Office, as well as common features they all share.

OBJECTIVES

Understand the Office 2010 suite

Start and exit an Office program

View the Office 2010 user interface

Create and save a file

Open a file and save it with a new name

View and print your work

Get Help and close a file

Understanding the Office 2010 Suite

Microsoft Office 2010 features an intuitive, context-sensitive user interface, so you can get up to speed faster and use advanced features with greater ease. The programs in Office are bundled together in a group called a **suite** (although you can also purchase them separately). The Office suite is available in several configurations, but all include Word, Excel, and PowerPoint. Other configurations include Access, Outlook, Publisher, and other programs. Each program in Office is best suited for completing specific types of tasks, though there is some overlap in capabilities.

DETAILS

The Office programs covered in this book include:

- **Microsoft Word 2010**

  When you need to create any kind of text-based document, such as a memo, newsletter, or multipage report, Word is the program to use. You can easily make your documents look great by inserting eye-catching graphics and using formatting tools such as themes, which are available in most Office programs. **Themes** are predesigned combinations of color and formatting attributes you can apply to a document. The Word document shown in Figure A-1 was formatted with the Solstice theme.

- **Microsoft Excel 2010**

  Excel is the perfect solution when you need to work with numeric values and make calculations. It puts the power of formulas, functions, charts, and other analytical tools into the hands of every user, so you can analyze sales projections, calculate loan payments, and present your findings in style. The Excel worksheet shown in Figure A-1 tracks personal expenses. Because Excel automatically recalculates results whenever a value changes, the information is always up to date. A chart illustrates how the monthly expenses are broken down.

- **Microsoft PowerPoint 2010**

  Using PowerPoint, it's easy to create powerful presentations complete with graphics, transitions, and even a soundtrack. Using professionally designed themes and clip art, you can quickly and easily create dynamic slide shows such as the one shown in Figure A-1.

- **Microsoft Access 2010**

  Access helps you keep track of large amounts of quantitative data, such as product inventories or employee records. The form shown in Figure A-1 was created for a grocery store inventory database. Employees use the form to enter data about each item. Using Access enables employees to quickly find specific information such as price and quantity without hunting through store shelves and stockrooms.

Microsoft Office has benefits beyond the power of each program, including:

- **Common user interface: Improving business processes**

  Because the Office suite programs have a similar **interface**, or look and feel, your experience using one program's tools makes it easy to learn those in the other programs. In addition, Office documents are **compatible** with one another, meaning that you can easily incorporate, or **integrate**, an Excel chart into a PowerPoint slide, or an Access table into a Word document.

- **Collaboration: Simplifying how people work together**

  Office recognizes the way people do business today, and supports the emphasis on communication and knowledge sharing within companies and across the globe. All Office programs include the capability to incorporate feedback—called **online collaboration**—across the Internet or a company network.

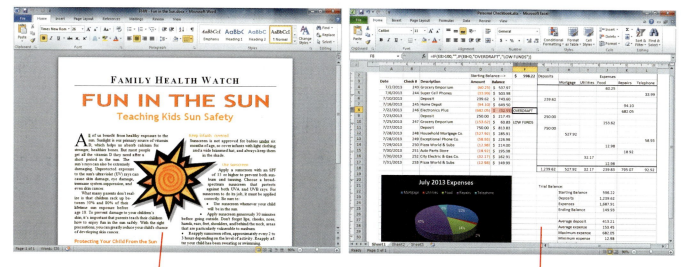

Newsletter created in Word

Checkbook register created in Excel

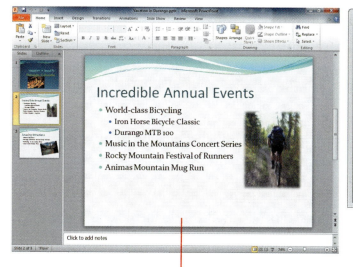

Tourism presentation created in PowerPoint

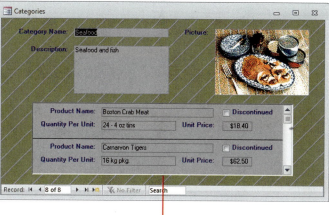

Store inventory form created in Access

Deciding which program to use

Every Office program includes tools that go far beyond what you might expect. For example, although Excel is primarily designed for making calculations, you can use it to create a database. So when you're planning a project, how do you decide which Office program to use? The general rule of thumb is to use the program best suited for your intended task, and make use of supporting tools in the program if you need them. Word is best for creating text-based documents, Excel is best for making mathematical calculations, PowerPoint is best for preparing presentations, and Access is best for managing quantitative data. Although the capabilities of Office are so vast that you *could* create an inventory in Excel or a budget in Word, you'll find greater flexibility and efficiency by using the program designed for the task. And remember, you can always create a file in one program, and then insert it in a document in another program when you need to, such as including sales projections (Excel) in a memo (Word).

Starting and Exiting an Office Program

The first step in using an Office program is to open, or **launch**, it on your computer. The easiest ways to launch a program are to click the Start button on the Windows taskbar or to double-click an icon on your desktop. You can have multiple programs open on your computer simultaneously, and you can move between open programs by clicking the desired program or document button on the taskbar or by using the [Alt][Tab] keyboard shortcut combination. When working, you'll often want to open multiple programs in Office and switch among them as you work. Begin by launching a few Office programs now.

STEPS

QUICK TIP

You can also launch a program by double-clicking a desktop icon or clicking the program name on the Start menu.

1. **Click the Start button 🏁 on the taskbar**

   The Start menu opens. If the taskbar is hidden, you can display it by pointing to the bottom of the screen. Depending on your taskbar property settings, the taskbar may be displayed at all times, or only when you point to that area of the screen. For more information, or to change your taskbar properties, consult your instructor or technical support person.

2. **Click All Programs, scroll down if necessary in the All Programs menu, click Microsoft Office as shown in Figure A-2, then click Microsoft Word 2010**

   Word 2010 starts, and the program window opens on your screen.

QUICK TIP

It is not necessary to close one program before opening another.

3. **Click 🏁 on the taskbar, click All Programs, click Microsoft Office, then click Microsoft Excel 2010**

   Excel 2010 starts, and the program window opens, as shown in Figure A-3. Word is no longer visible, but it remains open. The taskbar displays a button for each open program and document. Because this Excel document is **active**, or in front and available, the Excel button on the taskbar appears slightly lighter.

QUICK TIP

As you work in Windows, your computer adapts to your activities. You may notice that after clicking the Start button, the name of the program you want to open appears in the Start menu above All Programs; if so, you can click it to start the program.

4. **Point to the Word program button �W on the taskbar, then click �W**

   The Word program window is now in front. When the Aero feature is turned on in Windows 7, pointing to a program button on the taskbar displays a thumbnail version of each open window in that program above the program button. Clicking a program button on the taskbar activates that program and the most recently active document. Clicking a thumbnail of a document activates that document.

5. **Click 🏁 on the taskbar, click All Programs, click Microsoft Office, then click Microsoft PowerPoint 2010**

   PowerPoint 2010 starts and becomes the active program.

6. **Click the Excel program button 📊 on the taskbar**

   Excel is now the active program.

TROUBLE

If you don't have Access installed on your computer, proceed to the next lesson.

7. **Click 🏁 on the taskbar, click All Programs, click Microsoft Office, then click Microsoft Access 2010**

   Access 2010 starts and becomes the active program. Now all four Office programs are open at the same time.

8. **Click Exit on the navigation bar in the Access program window, as shown in Figure A-4**

   Access closes, leaving Excel active and Word and PowerPoint open.

Using shortcut keys to move between Office programs

As an alternative to the Windows taskbar, you can use a keyboard shortcut to move among open Office programs. The [Alt][Tab] keyboard combination lets you either switch quickly to the next open program or file or choose one from a gallery. To switch immediately to the next open program or file, press [Alt][Tab]. To choose from all open programs and files, press and hold [Alt], then press and release [Tab] without releasing [Alt]. A gallery opens on screen, displaying the filename and a thumbnail image of each open program and file, as well as of the desktop. Each time you press [Tab] while holding [Alt], the selection cycles to the next open file or location. Release [Alt] when the program, file, or location you want to activate is selected.

FIGURE A-2: Start menu

All programs
menu (yours
will look
different)

Start button   Taskbar

FIGURE A-3: Excel program window and Windows taskbar

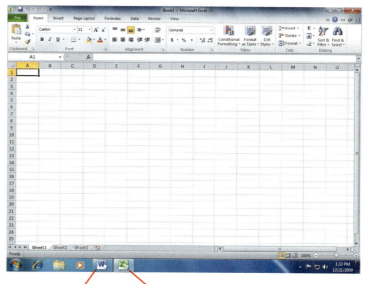

Word program
button on the
taskbar

Excel program
button on the
taskbar

FIGURE A-4: Access program window

File tab

Navigation bar

Exit command

Windows Live and Microsoft Office Web Apps

All Office programs include the capability to incorporate feedback—called online collaboration—across the Internet or a company network. Using **cloud computing** (work done in a virtual environment), you can take advantage of Web programs called Microsoft Office Web Apps, which are simplified versions of the programs found in the Microsoft Office 2010 suite. Because these programs are online, they take up no computer disk space and are accessed using Windows Live SkyDrive, a free service from Microsoft. Using Windows Live SkyDrive, you and your colleagues can create and store documents in a "cloud" and make the documents available to whomever you grant access. To use Windows Live SkyDrive, you need a free Windows Live ID, which you obtain at the Windows Live Web site. You can find more information in the "Working with Windows Live and Office Web Apps" appendix.

Viewing the Office 2010 User Interface

One of the benefits of using Office is that the programs have much in common, making them easy to learn and making it simple to move from one to another. Individual Office programs have always shared many features, but the innovations in the Office 2010 user interface mean even greater similarity among them all. That means you can also use your knowledge of one program to get up to speed in another. A **user interface** is a collective term for all the ways you interact with a software program. The user interface in Office 2010 provides intuitive ways to choose commands, work with files, and navigate in the program window. Familiarize yourself with some of the common interface elements in Office by examining the PowerPoint program window.

STEPS

1. **Click the PowerPoint program button 📷 on the taskbar**

   PowerPoint becomes the active program. Refer to Figure A-5 to identify common elements of the Office user interface. The **document window** occupies most of the screen. In PowerPoint, a blank slide appears in the document window, so you can build your slide show. At the top of every Office program window is a **title bar** that displays the document name and program name. Below the title bar is the **Ribbon**, which displays commands you're likely to need for the current task. Commands are organized onto **tabs**. The tab names appear at the top of the Ribbon, and the active tab appears in front. The Ribbon in every Office program includes tabs specific to the program, but all Office programs include a File tab and Home tab on the left end of the Ribbon.

2. **Click the File tab**

   The File tab opens, displaying **Backstage view**. The navigation bar on the left side of Backstage view contains commands to perform actions common to most Office programs, such as opening a file, saving a file, and closing the current program. Just above the File tab is the **Quick Access toolbar**, which also includes buttons for common Office commands.

3. **Click the File tab again to close Backstage view and return to the document window, then click the Design tab on the Ribbon**

   To display a different tab, you click the tab on the Ribbon. Each tab contains related commands arranged into **groups** to make features easy to find. On the Design tab, the Themes group displays available design themes in a **gallery**, or visual collection of choices you can browse. Many groups contain a **dialog box launcher**, an icon you can click to open a dialog box or task pane from which to choose related commands.

4. **Move the mouse pointer ⌖ over the Angles theme in the Themes group as shown in Figure A-6, but do not click the mouse button**

   The Angles theme is temporarily applied to the slide in the document window. However, because you did not click the theme, you did not permanently change the slide. With the **Live Preview** feature, you can point to a choice, see the results right in the document, and then decide if you want to make the change.

5. **Move ⌖ away from the Ribbon and towards the slide**

   If you had clicked the Angles theme, it would be applied to this slide. Instead, the slide remains unchanged.

6. **Point to the Zoom slider ▽ on the status bar, then drag ▽ to the right until the Zoom level reads 166%**

   The slide display is enlarged. Zoom tools are located on the status bar. You can drag the slider or click the Zoom In or Zoom Out buttons to zoom in or out on an area of interest. **Zooming in**, or choosing a higher percentage, makes a document appear bigger on screen, but less of it fits on the screen at once; **zooming out**, or choosing a lower percentage, lets you see more of the document but at a reduced size.

7. **Drag ▽ on the status bar to the left until the Zoom level reads 73%**

FIGURE A-5: PowerPoint program window

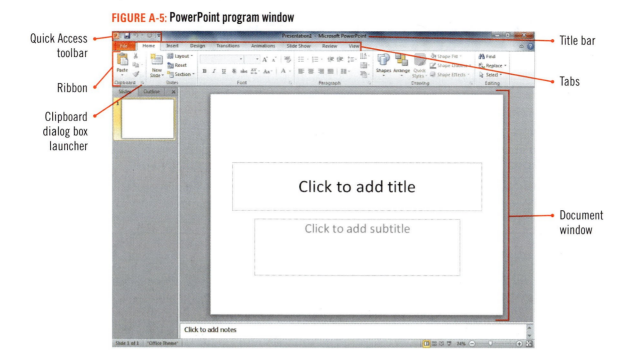

Quick Access toolbar

Ribbon

Clipboard dialog box launcher

Title bar

Tabs

Document window

FIGURE A-6: Viewing a theme with Live Preview

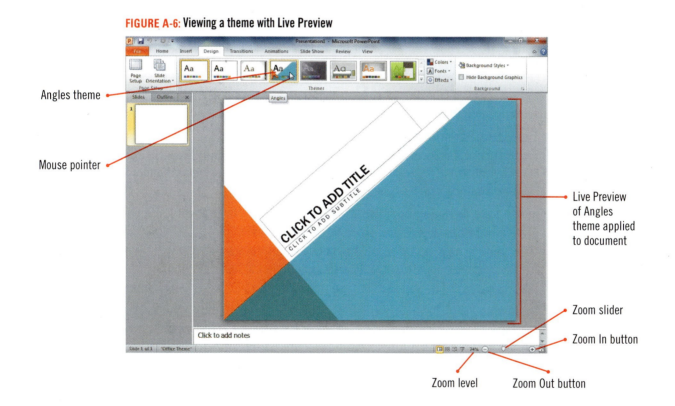

Angles theme

Mouse pointer

Live Preview of Angles theme applied to document

Zoom slider

Zoom In button

Zoom level

Zoom Out button

Using Backstage view

Backstage view in each Microsoft Office program offers "one stop shopping" for many commonly performed tasks, such as opening and saving a file, printing and previewing a document, defining document properties, sharing information, and exiting a program.

Backstage view opens when you click the File tab in any Office program, and while features such as the Ribbon, Mini toolbar, and Live Preview all help you work *in* your documents, the File tab and Backstage view help you work *with* your documents.

Creating and Saving a File

When working in a program, one of the first things you need to do is to create and save a file. A **file** is a stored collection of data. Saving a file enables you to work on a project now, then put it away and work on it again later. In some Office programs, including Word, Excel, and PowerPoint, a new file is automatically created when you start the program, so all you have to do is enter some data and save it. In Access, you must expressly create a file before you enter any data. You should give your files meaningful names and save them in an appropriate location so that they're easy to find. Use Word to familiarize yourself with the process of creating and saving a document. First you'll type some notes about a possible location for a corporate meeting, then you'll save the information for later use.

STEPS

1. **Click the Word program button 🔳 on the taskbar**

2. **Type Locations for Corporate Meeting, then press [Enter] twice**
   The text appears in the document window, and the **insertion point** blinks on a new blank line. The insertion point indicates where the next typed text will appear.

3. **Type Las Vegas, NV, press [Enter], type Orlando, FL, press [Enter], type Boston, MA, press [Enter] twice, then type your name**
   Compare your document to Figure A-7.

> **QUICK TIP**
>
> A filename can be up to 255 characters, including a file extension, and can include upper- or lowercase characters and spaces, but not ?, ", /, \, <, >, *, |, or :.

4. **Click the Save button 🔲 on the Quick Access toolbar**
   Because this is the first time you are saving this document, the Save As dialog box opens, as shown in Figure A-8. The Save As dialog box includes options for assigning a filename and storage location. Once you save a file for the first time, clicking 🔲 saves any changes to the file *without* opening the Save As dialog box, because no additional information is needed. The Address bar in the Save As dialog box displays the default location for saving the file, but you can change it to any location. The File name field contains a suggested name for the document based on text in the file, but you can enter a different name.

5. **Type OF A-Potential Corporate Meeting Locations**
   The text you type replaces the highlighted text. (The "OF A-" in the filename indicates that the file is created in Office Unit A. You will see similar designations throughout this book when files are named. For example, a file named in Excel Unit B would begin with "EX B-".)

> **QUICK TIP**
>
> Saving a file to the Desktop creates a desktop icon that you can double-click to both launch a program and open a document.

6. **In the Save As dialog box, use the Address bar or Navigation Pane to navigate to the drive and folder where you store your Data Files**
   Many students store files on a flash drive, but you can also store files on your computer, a network drive, or any storage device indicated by your instructor or technical support person.

> **QUICK TIP**
>
> To create a new blank file when a file is open, click the File tab, click New on the navigation bar, then click Create near the bottom of the document preview pane.

7. **Click Save**
   The Save As dialog box closes, the new file is saved to the location you specified, then the name of the document appears in the title bar, as shown in Figure A-9. (You may or may not see the file extension ".docx" after the filename.) See Table A-1 for a description of the different types of files you create in Office, and the file extensions associated with each.

TABLE A-1: Common filenames and default file extensions

file created in	is called a	and has the default extension
Word	document	.docx
Excel	workbook	.xlsx
PowerPoint	presentation	.pptx
Access	database	.accdb

Save button

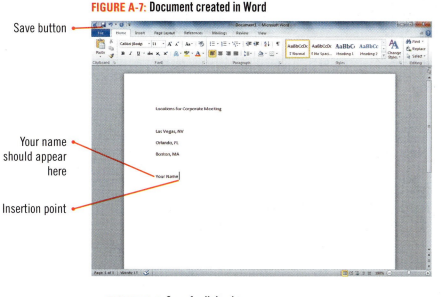

Your name should appear here

Insertion point

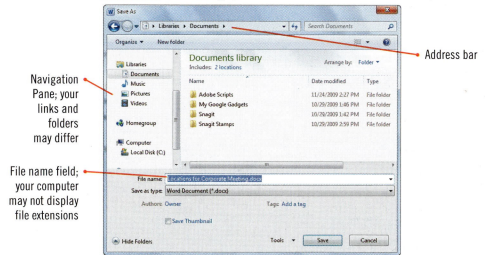

Address bar

Navigation Pane; your links and folders may differ

File name field; your computer may not display file extensions

Filename appears in title bar

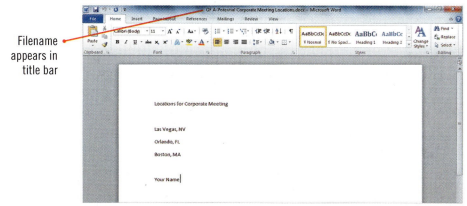

Using the Office Clipboard

You can use the Office Clipboard to cut and copy items from one Office program and paste them into others. The Office Clipboard can store a maximum of 24 items. To access it, open the Office Clipboard task pane by clicking the dialog box launcher  in the Clipboard group on the Home tab. Each time you copy a selection, it is saved in the Office Clipboard. Each entry in the Office Clipboard includes an icon that tells you the program it was created in. To paste an entry, click in the document where you want it to appear, then click the item in the Office Clipboard. To delete an item from the Office Clipboard, right-click the item, then click Delete.

Opening a File and Saving It with a New Name

In many cases as you work in Office, you start with a blank document, but often you need to use an existing file. It might be a file you or a coworker created earlier as a work in progress, or it could be a complete document that you want to use as the basis for another. For example, you might want to create a budget for this year using the budget you created last year; you could type in all the categories and information from scratch, or you could open last year's budget, save it with a new name, and just make changes to update it for the current year. By opening the existing file and saving it with the Save As command, you create a duplicate that you can modify to your heart's content, while the original file remains intact. Use Excel to open an existing workbook file, and save it with a new name so the original remains unchanged.

STEPS

QUICK TIP
Click Recent on the navigation bar to display a list of recent workbooks; click a file in the list to open it.

1. **Click the Excel program button 🟩 on the taskbar, click the File tab, then click Open on the navigation bar**

   The Open dialog box opens, where you can navigate to any drive or folder accessible to your computer to locate a file.

2. **In the Open dialog box, navigate to the drive and folder where you store your Data Files**

   The files available in the current folder are listed, as shown in Figure A-10. This folder contains one file.

TROUBLE
Click Enable Editing on the Protected View bar near the top of your document window if prompted.

3. **Click OFFICE A-1.xlsx, then click Open**

   The dialog box closes, and the file opens in Excel. An Excel file is an electronic spreadsheet, so it looks different from a Word document or a PowerPoint slide.

4. **Click the File tab, then click Save As on the navigation bar**

   The Save As dialog box opens, and the current filename is highlighted in the File name text box. Using the Save As command enables you to create a copy of the current, existing file with a new name. This action preserves the original file and creates a new file that you can modify.

QUICK TIP
The Save As command works identically in all Office programs, except Access; in Access, this command lets you save a copy of the current database object, such as a table or form, with a new name, but not a copy of the entire database.

5. **Navigate to the drive and folder where you store your Data Files if necessary, type OF A-Budget for Corporate Meeting in the File name text box, as shown in Figure A-11, then click Save**

   A copy of the existing workbook is created with the new name. The original file, Office A-1.xlsx, closes automatically.

6. **Click cell A19, type your name, then press [Enter], as shown in Figure A-12**

   In Excel, you enter data in cells, which are formed by the intersection of a row and a column. Cell A19 is at the intersection of column A and row 19. When you press [Enter], the cell pointer moves to cell A20.

7. **Click the Save button 🖫 on the Quick Access toolbar**

   Your name appears in the workbook, and your changes to the file are saved.

Working in Compatibility Mode

Not everyone upgrades to the newest version of Office. As a general rule, new software versions are **backward compatible**, meaning that documents saved by an older version can be read by newer software. To open documents created in older Office versions, Office 2010 includes a feature called Compatibility Mode. When you use Office 2010 to open a file created in an earlier version of Office, "Compatibility Mode" appears in the title bar, letting you know the file was created in an earlier but usable version of the program. If you are working with someone who may not be using the newest version of the software, you can avoid possible incompatibility problems by saving your file in another, earlier format. To do this in an Office program, click the File tab, click Save As on the navigation bar, click the Save as type list arrow in the Save As dialog box, then click an option on the list. For example, if you're working in Excel, click Excel 97-2003 Workbook format in the Save as type list to save an Excel file so that it can be opened in Excel 97 or Excel 2003.

FIGURE A-10: Open dialog box

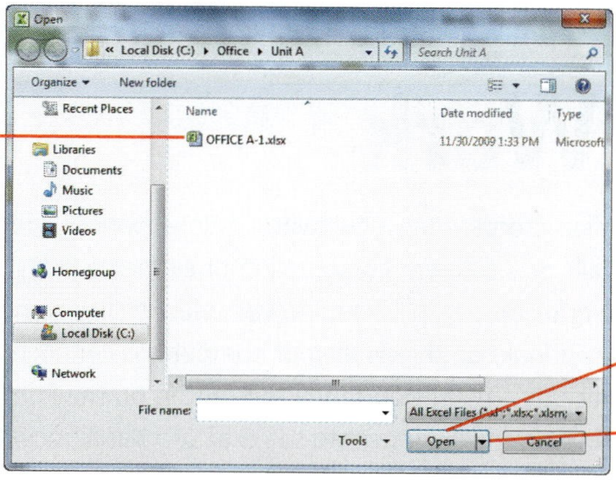

Available files in this folder

Open button

Open list arrow

FIGURE A-11: Save As dialog box

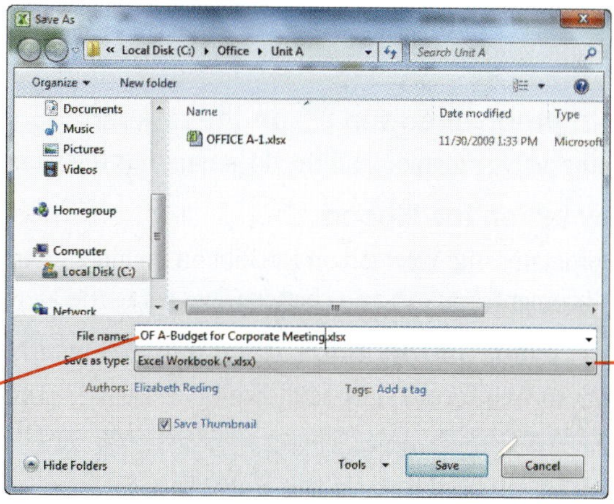

New filename

Save as type list arrow

FIGURE A-12: Your name added to the workbook

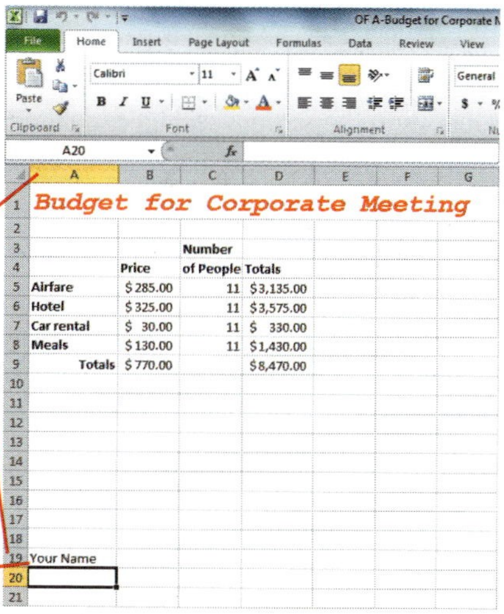

Address for cell A19 formed by column A and row 19

Cell A19; type your name here

Exploring File Open options

You might have noticed that the Open button on the Open dialog box includes an arrow. In a dialog box, if a button includes an arrow you can click the button to invoke the command, or you can click the arrow to choose from a list of related commands. The Open list arrow includes several related commands, including Open Read-Only and Open as Copy. Clicking Open Read-Only opens a file that you can only save with a new name; you cannot save changes to the original file. Clicking Open as Copy creates a copy of the file already saved and named with the word "Copy" in the title. Like the Save As command, these commands provide additional ways to use copies of existing files while ensuring that original files do not get changed by mistake.

Viewing and Printing Your Work

Each Microsoft Office program lets you switch among various **views** of the document window to show more or fewer details or a different combination of elements that make it easier to complete certain tasks, such as formatting or reading text. Changing your view of a document does not affect the file in any way, it affects only the way it looks on screen. If your computer is connected to a printer or a print server, you can easily print any Office document using the Print button on the Print tab in Backstage view. Printing can be as simple as **previewing** the document to see exactly what a document will look like when it is printed and then clicking the Print button. Or, you can customize the print job by printing only selected pages or making other choices. Experiment with changing your view of a Word document, and then preview and print your work.

STEPS

1. **Click the Word program button [W] on the taskbar**

   Word becomes the active program, and the document fills the screen.

2. **Click the View tab on the Ribbon**

   In most Office programs, the View tab on the Ribbon includes groups and commands for changing your view of the current document. You can also change views using the View buttons on the status bar.

3. **Click the Web Layout button in the Document Views group on the View tab**

   The view changes to Web Layout view, as shown in Figure A-13. This view shows how the document will look if you save it as a Web page.

4. **Click the Print Layout button on the View tab**

   You return to Print Layout view, the default view in Word.

5. **Click the File tab, then click Print on the navigation bar**

   The Print tab opens in Backstage view. The preview pane on the right side of the window automatically displays a preview of how your document will look when printed, showing the entire page on screen at once. Compare your screen to Figure A-14. Options in the Settings section enable you to change settings such as margins, orientation, and paper size before printing. To change a setting, click it, and then click the new setting you want. For instance, to change from Letter paper size to Legal, click Letter in the Settings section, then click Legal on the menu that opens. The document preview is updated as you change the settings. You also can use the Settings section to change which pages to print and even the number of pages you print on each sheet of printed paper. If you have multiple printers from which to choose, you can change from one installed printer to another by clicking the current printer in the Printer section, then clicking the name of the installed printer you want to use. The Print section contains the Print button and also enables you to select the number of copies of the document to print.

6. **Click the Print button in the Print section**

   A copy of the document prints, and Backstage view closes.

> **QUICK TIP**
> You can add the Quick Print button to the Quick Access toolbar by clicking the Customize Quick Access Toolbar button, then clicking Quick Print. The Quick Print button prints one copy of your document using the default settings.

Customizing the Quick Access toolbar

You can customize the Quick Access toolbar to display your favorite commands. To do so, click the Customize Quick Access Toolbar button in the title bar, then click the command you want to add. If you don't see the command in the list, click More Commands to open the Quick Access Toolbar tab of the current program's Options dialog box. In the Options dialog box, use the Choose commands from list to choose a category, click the desired command in the list on the left, click Add to add it to the Quick Access toolbar, then click

OK. To remove a button from the toolbar, click the name in the list on the right in the Options dialog box, then click Remove. To add a command to the Quick Access toolbar on the fly, simply right-click the button on the Ribbon, then click Add to Quick Access Toolbar on the shortcut menu. To move the Quick Access toolbar below the Ribbon, click the Customize Quick Access Toolbar button, and then click Show Below the Ribbon.

FIGURE A-13: Web Layout view

Web Layout button

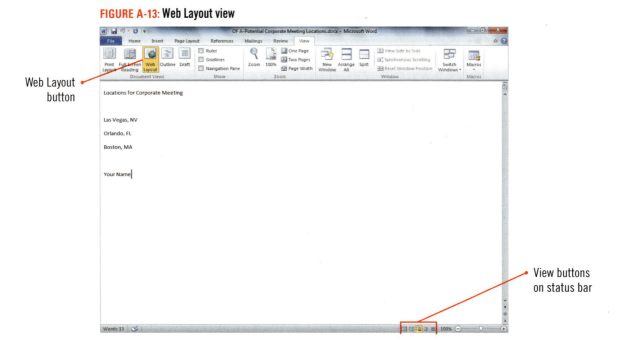

View buttons on status bar

FIGURE A-14: Print tab in Backstage view

Print button

Click to select a different installed printer

Settings section

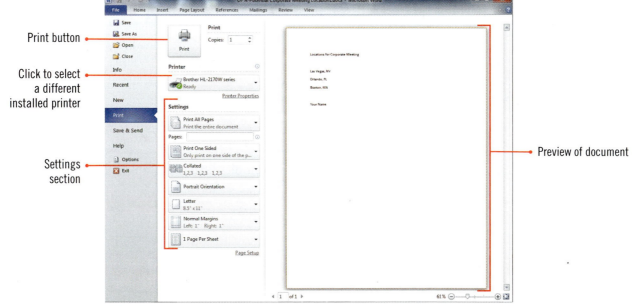

Preview of document

Getting Help and Closing a File

You can get comprehensive help at any time by pressing [F1] in an Office program. You can also get help in the form of a ScreenTip by pointing to almost any icon in the program window. When you're finished working in an Office document, you have a few choices regarding ending your work session. You can close a file or exit a program by using the File tab or by clicking a button on the title bar. Closing a file leaves a program running, while exiting a program closes all the open files in that program as well as the program itself. In all cases, Office reminds you if you try to close a file or exit a program and your document contains unsaved changes. Explore the Help system in Microsoft Office, and then close your documents and exit any open programs.

STEPS

TROUBLE

If the Table of Contents pane doesn't appear on the left in the Help window, click the Show Table of Contents button on the Help toolbar to show it.

QUICK TIP

You can also open the Help window by clicking the Microsoft Office Word Help button to the right of the tabs on the Ribbon.

QUICK TIP

You can print the entire current topic by clicking the Print button on the Help toolbar, then clicking Print in the Print dialog box.

1. **Point to the Zoom button on the View tab of the Ribbon**

   A ScreenTip appears that describes how the Zoom button works and explains where to find other zoom controls.

2. **Press [F1]**

   The Word Help window opens, as shown in Figure A-15, displaying the home page for help in Word on the right and the Table of Contents pane on the left. In both panes of the Help window, each entry is a hyperlink you can click to open a list of related topics. The Help window also includes a toolbar of useful Help commands and a Search field. The connection status at the bottom of the Help window indicates that the connection to Office.com is active. Office.com supplements the help content available on your computer with a wide variety of up-to-date topics, templates, and training. If you are not connected to the Internet, the Help window displays only the help content available on your computer.

3. **Click the Creating documents link in the Table of Contents pane**

   The icon next to Creating documents changes, and a list of subtopics expands beneath the topic.

4. **Click the Create a document link in the subtopics list in the Table of Contents pane**

   The topic opens in the right pane of the Help window, as shown in Figure A-16.

5. **Click Delete a document under "What do you want to do?" in the right pane**

   The link leads to information about deleting a document.

6. **Click the Accessibility link in the Table of Contents pane, click the Accessibility features in Word link, read the information in the right pane, then click the Help window Close button**

7. **Click the File tab, then click Close on the navigation bar; if a dialog box opens asking whether you want to save your changes, click Save**

   The Potential Corporate Meeting Locations document closes, leaving the Word program open.

8. **Click the File tab, then click Exit on the navigation bar**

   Word closes, and the Excel program window is active.

9. **Click the File tab, click Exit on the navigation bar to exit Excel, click the PowerPoint program button on the taskbar if necessary, click the File tab, then click Exit on the navigation bar to exit PowerPoint**

   Excel and PowerPoint both close.

FIGURE A-15: Word Help window

Help toolbar

Search field

The colors of
your links may
differ if the
links have
been visited
previously

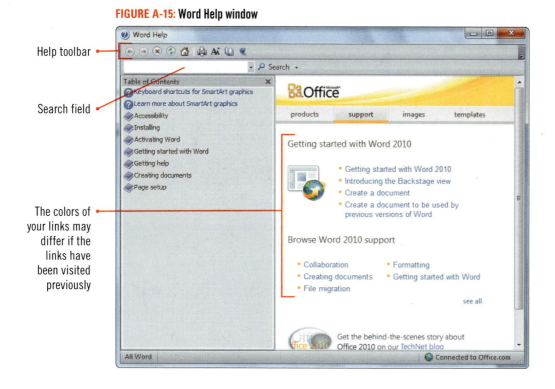

FIGURE A-16: Create a document Help topic

Print button

Icon indicates
expanded topic

Create a
document link

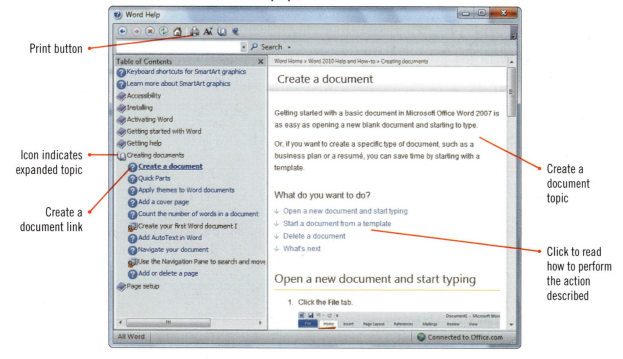

Create a
document
topic

Click to read
how to perform
the action
described

Recovering a document

Each Office program has a built-in recovery feature that allows you to open and save files that were open at the time of an interruption such as a power failure. When you restart the program(s) after an interruption, the Document Recovery task pane opens on the left side of your screen displaying both original and recovered versions of the files that were open. If you're not sure which file to open (original or recovered), it's usually better to open the recovered file because it will contain the latest information. You can, however, open and review all versions of the file that were recovered and save the best one. Each file listed in the Document Recovery task pane displays a list arrow with options that allow you to open the file, save it as is, delete it, or show repairs made to it during recovery.

Practice

SAM

For current SAM information, including versions and content details, visit SAM Central (http://www.cengage.com/samcentral). If you have a SAM user profile, you may have access to hands-on instruction, practice, and assessment of the skills covered in this unit. Since various versions of SAM are supported throughout the life of this text, check with your instructor for the correct instructions and URL/Web site for accessing assignments.

Concepts Review

Label the elements of the program window shown in Figure A-17.

FIGURE A-17

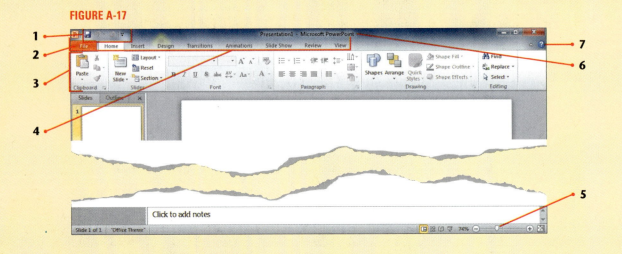

Match each project with the program for which it is best suited.

8. Microsoft Access

9. Microsoft Excel

10. Microsoft Word

11. Microsoft PowerPoint

a. Corporate convention budget with expense projections

b. Business cover letter for a job application

c. Department store inventory

d. Presentation for city council meeting

Independent Challenge 1

You just accepted an administrative position with a local independently owned produce vendor that has recently invested in computers and is now considering purchasing Microsoft Office for the company. You are asked to propose ways Office might help the business. You produce your document in Word.

a. Start Word, then save the document as **OF A-Microsoft Office Document** in the drive and folder where you store your Data Files.

b. Type **Microsoft Word**, press [Enter] twice, type **Microsoft Excel**, press [Enter] twice, type **Microsoft PowerPoint**, press [Enter] twice, type **Microsoft Access**, press [Enter] twice, then type your name.

c. Click the line beneath each program name, type at least two tasks suited to that program (each separated by a comma), then press [Enter].

Advanced Challenge Exercise

- Press the [PrtScn] button to create a screen capture.
- Click after your name, press [Enter] to move to a blank line below your name, then click the Paste button in the Clipboard group on the Home tab.

d. Save the document, then submit your work to your instructor as directed.

e. Exit Word.

Creating a Presentation in PowerPoint 2010

Microsoft PowerPoint 2010 is a powerful computer software program that enables you to create visually dynamic presentations. With PowerPoint, you can create individual slides and display them as a slide show on your computer, a video projector, or over the Internet. 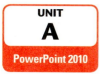 Quest Specialty Travel (QST) is an adventure tour company dedicated to providing exclusive and unique cultural travel experiences for its clients. As a sales associate for QST, one of your responsibilities is to research new vacation tours throughout North America, including Canada and Alaska, that QST can sell over the Internet using the company Web site. You have just finished investigating Canadian train travel, and now you need to create a presentation using PowerPoint 2010 that describes the results of your research.

OBJECTIVES

Define presentation software

Plan an effective presentation

Examine the PowerPoint window

Enter slide text

Add a new slide

Apply a design theme

Compare presentation views

Print a PowerPoint presentation

Defining Presentation Software

Presentation software is a computer program you use to organize and present information to others. Whether you are explaining a new product or moderating a meeting, presentation software can help you effectively communicate your ideas. You can use PowerPoint to create presentations, as well as speaker notes for the presenter and handouts for the audience. Table A-1 explains how your information can be presented using PowerPoint. You need to start work on the presentation you will use to present the new Canadian train tours. Because you are only somewhat familiar with PowerPoint, you get to work exploring its capabilities. Figure A-1 shows how a presentation looks printed as handouts. Figure A-2 shows how the same presentation might look printed as notes for a speaker.

DETAILS

You can easily complete the following tasks using PowerPoint:

• **Enter and edit text easily**
Text editing and formatting commands in PowerPoint are organized by the task you are performing at the time, so you can enter, edit, and format text information simply and efficiently to produce the best results in the least amount of time.

• **Change the appearance of information**
PowerPoint has many effects that can transform the way text, graphics, and slides appear. By exploring some of these capabilities, you discover how easy it is to change the appearance of your presentation.

• **Organize and arrange information**
Once you start using PowerPoint, you won't have to spend much time making sure your information is correct and in the right order. With PowerPoint, you can quickly and easily rearrange and modify text, graphics, and slides in your presentation.

• **Incorporate information from other sources**
Often, when you create presentations, you use information from a variety of sources. With PowerPoint, you can import text, photographs, numerical data, and facts from files created in programs such as Microsoft Word, Corel WordPerfect, Adobe Photoshop, Microsoft Excel, and Microsoft Access. You can also import graphic images from a variety of sources such as the Internet, other computers, a digital camera, or other graphics programs. Always be sure you have permission to use any work that you did not create yourself.

• **Present information in a variety of ways**
With PowerPoint, you can present information using a variety of methods. For example, you can print handout pages or an outline of your presentation for audience members. You can display your presentation as an on-screen slide show using your computer, or if you are presenting to a large group, you can use a video projector and a large screen. If you want to reach an even wider audience, you can broadcast the presentation over the Internet so people anywhere in the world can use a Web browser to view your presentation.

• **Collaborate on a presentation with others**
PowerPoint makes it easy to collaborate or share a presentation with colleagues and coworkers using the Internet. You can use your e-mail program to send a presentation as an attachment to a colleague for feedback. If you have a number of people that need to work together on a presentation, you can save the presentation to a shared workspace on the Internet so everyone in your group using a Web browser has access to the presentation.

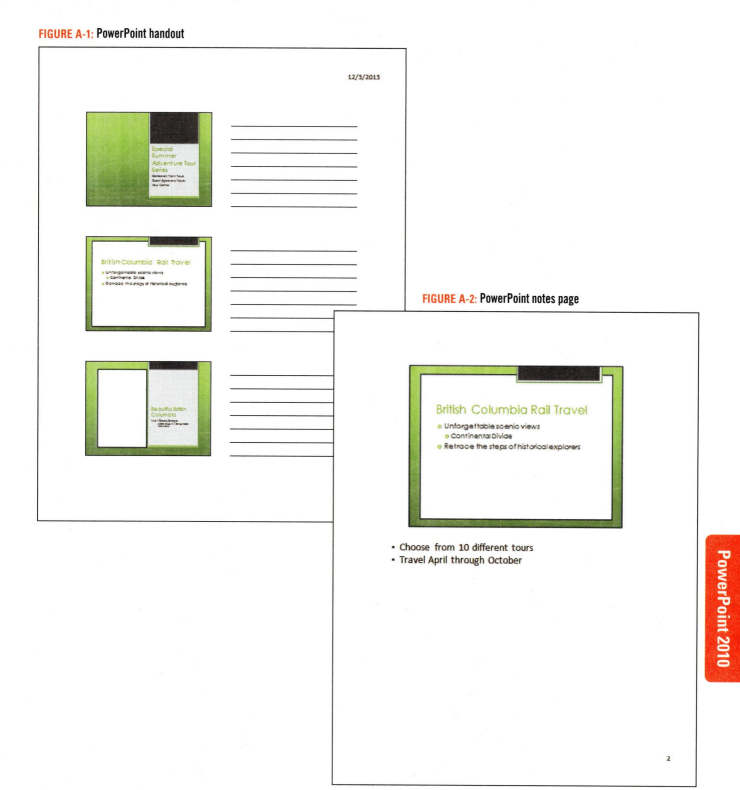

FIGURE A-1: PowerPoint handout

FIGURE A-2: PowerPoint notes page

TABLE A-1: Presenting information using PowerPoint

method	description
On-screen presentations	Run a slide show from your computer or through a video projector to a large screen
Notes	Print a page with the image of a slide and notes about each slide for yourself or your audience
Audience handouts	Print handouts with one, two, three, four, six, or nine slides on a page
Broadcast a slide show	Broadcast a slide show to other viewers who watch using a Web browser
Outline pages	Print a text outline of your presentation to highlight the main points

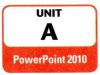

Planning an Effective Presentation

Before you create a presentation, you need to have a general idea of the information you want to communicate. PowerPoint is a powerful and flexible program that gives you the ability to start a presentation simply by entering the text of your message. If you have a specific design or theme you want to use, you can start the presentation by working on the design. In most cases you'll probably enter the text of your presentation into PowerPoint first and then tailor the design to the message and audience. When preparing your presentation, you need to keep in mind not only who you are giving it to, but also where you are giving it. It is important to know what equipment you will need, such as a sound system, computer, or projector. Use the planning guidelines below to help plan an effective presentation. Figure A-3 illustrates a storyboard for a well-planned presentation.

DETAILS

In planning a presentation, it is important to:

- **Determine and outline the message you want to communicate**

  The more time you take developing the message and outline of your presentation, the better your presentation will be in the end. A presentation with a clear message that reads like a story and is illustrated with appropriate visual aids will have the greatest impact on your audience. Start the presentation by giving a general description of Canadian train travel and the types of tours offered by Quest Speciality Travel. See Figure A-3.

- **Identify your audience and delivery location**

  Audience and delivery location are major factors in the type of presentation you create. For example, a presentation you develop for a staff meeting that is held in a conference room would not necessarily need to be as sophisticated or detailed as a presentation that you develop for a large audience held in an auditorium. Room lighting, natural light, screen position, and room layout all affect how the audience responds to your presentation. This presentation will be delivered in a small auditorium to QST's management and sales team.

- **Determine the type of output**

  Output choices for a presentation include black-and-white or color handouts, on-screen slide show, or an online broadcast. Consider the time demands and computer equipment availability as you decide which output types to produce. Because you are speaking in a small auditorium to a large group and have access to a computer and projection equipment, you decide that an on-screen slide show is the best output choice for your presentation.

- **Determine the design**

  Visual appeal, graphics, and presentation design work to communicate your message. You can choose one of the professionally designed themes that come with PowerPoint, modify one of these themes, or create one of your own. You decide to choose one of PowerPoint's design themes to convey the new tour information.

- **Decide what additional materials will be useful in the presentation**

  You need to prepare not only the slides themselves but also supplementary materials, including speaker notes and handouts for the audience. You use speaker notes to help remember key details, and you pass out handouts for the audience to use as a reference during the presentation.

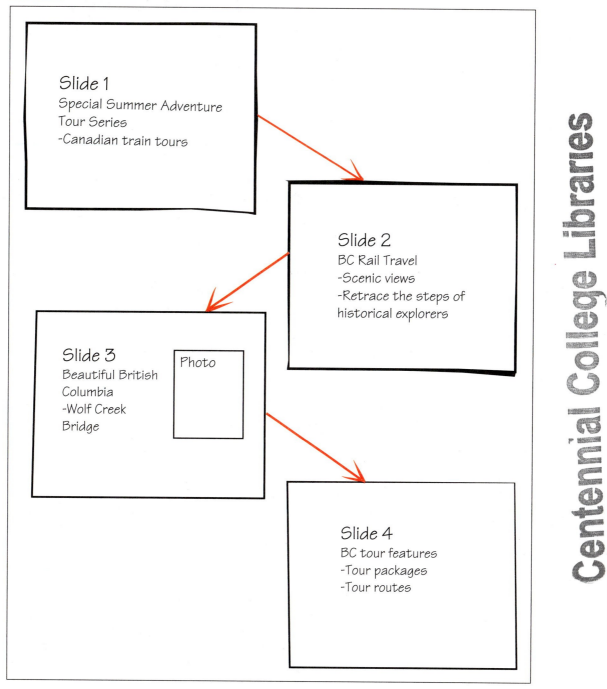

Centennial College Libraries

Understanding copyright

Intellectual property is any idea or creation of the human mind. Copyright law is a type of intellectual property law that protects works of authorship, including books, Web pages, computer games, music, artwork, and photographs. Copyright protects the expression of an idea, but not the underlying facts or concepts. In other words, the general subject matter is not protected, but how you express it *is*, such as when several people photograph the same sunset. Copyright attaches to any original work of authorship *as soon* as it is created, you do not have to register it with the Copyright Office or display the copyright symbol, ©.

Fair use is an exception to copyright and permits the public to use copyrighted material for certain purposes without obtaining prior consent from the owner. Determining whether fair use applies to a work depends on its purpose, the nature of the work, how much of the work you want to copy, and the effect on the work's value. Unauthorized use of protected work (such as downloading a photo or a song from the Web) is known as copyright infringement and can lead to legal action.

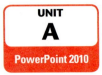
Examining the PowerPoint Window

When you first start PowerPoint, a blank slide appears in the PowerPoint window. PowerPoint has different **views** that allow you to see your presentation in different forms. By default, the PowerPoint window opens in **Normal view**, which is the primary view that you use to write, edit, and design your presentation. Normal view is divided into three areas called **panes**: the pane on the left contains the Outline and Slides tabs, the large pane is the Slide pane, and the small pane below the Slide pane is the Notes pane. You move around in each pane using the scroll bars. ▒▒▒▒ The PowerPoint window and the specific parts of Normal view are described below.

STEPS

TROUBLE

If you have trouble finding Microsoft PowerPoint 2010 on the All Programs menu, check with your instructor or technical support person.

1. **Click the Start button 🪟 on the taskbar, click All Programs, click Microsoft Office, then click Microsoft PowerPoint 2010**
   PowerPoint starts and the PowerPoint window opens, as shown in Figure A-4.

Using Figure A-4 as a guide, examine the elements of the PowerPoint window, then find and compare the elements described below:

- The **Ribbon** is a wide (toolbar-like) band that runs across the entire PowerPoint window that organizes all of PowerPoint's primary commands. Each set of primary commands is identified by a **tab**; for example, the Home tab is selected by default, as shown in Figure A-4. Commands are further arranged into **groups** on the Ribbon based on their function. So, for example, text formatting commands such as Bold, Underline, and Italic are located on the Home tab, in the Font group.

- The **Outline tab** displays the text of your presentation in the form of an outline, without showing graphics or other visual objects. Using this tab, it is easy to move text on or among slides by dragging text to reorder the information.

- The **Slides tab** displays the slides of your presentation as small images, called **thumbnails**. You can quickly navigate through the slides in your presentation by clicking the thumbnails on this tab. You can also add, delete, or rearrange slides using this tab.

- The **Slide pane** displays the current slide in your presentation.

- The **Notes pane** is used to type text that references a slide's content. You can print these notes and refer to them when you make a presentation or print them as handouts and give them to your audience. The Notes pane is not visible to the audience when you show a slide presentation in Slide Show view.

- The **Quick Access toolbar** provides access to common commands such as Save, Undo, and Redo. The Quick Access toolbar is always visible no matter which Ribbon tab you select. This toolbar is fully customizable. Click the Customize Quick Access Toolbar button to add or remove commands.

- The **View Shortcuts** icons on the status bar allow you to switch quickly between PowerPoint views.

- The **status bar**, located at the bottom of the PowerPoint window, shows messages about what you are doing and seeing in PowerPoint, including which slide you are viewing, and the design theme applied to the presentation. In addition, the status bar displays the Zoom slider controls, the Fit slide to current window button 🔲, and information on other functionality such as signatures and permissions.

- The **Zoom slider** is in the lower-right corner of the status bar, use to zoom the slide in and out quickly.

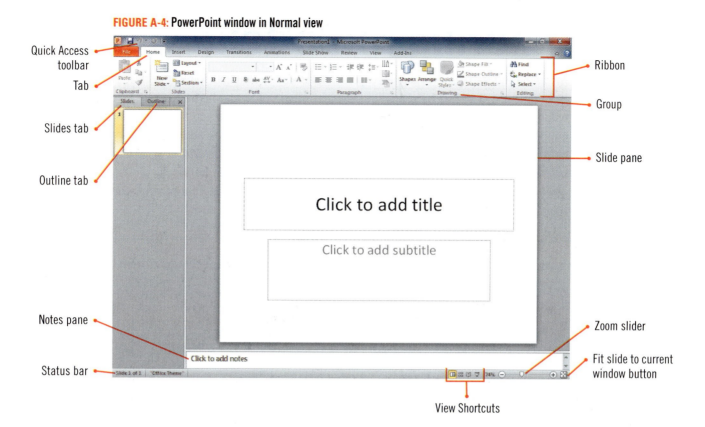

FIGURE A-4: PowerPoint window in Normal view

Quick Access toolbar
Tab
Slides tab
Outline tab
Notes pane
Status bar
Ribbon
Group
Slide pane
Zoom slider
Fit slide to current window button
View Shortcuts

Click to add title

Click to add subtitle

Click to add notes

Viewing your presentation in grayscale or black and white

Viewing your presentation in grayscale (using shades of gray) or pure black and white is very useful when you are printing a presentation on a black-and-white printer and you want to make sure your presentation prints correctly. To see how your color presentation looks in grayscale or black and white, click the View tab, then click either the Grayscale or Black and White button in the Color/Grayscale group. Depending on which button you select, the Grayscale or the Black and White tab appears, and the Ribbon displays different settings that you can customize. If you don't like the way an individual object looks in black and white or grayscale, you can change its color. Click the object while still in Grayscale or Black and White view, then choose an option in the Change Selected Object group on the Ribbon.

Entering Slide Text

Each time you start PowerPoint, a new presentation with a blank title slide appears in Normal view. The title slide has two **text placeholders**—boxes with dotted borders—where you enter text. The top text placeholder on the title slide is the **title placeholder**, labeled "Click to add title." The bottom text placeholder on the title slide is the **subtitle text placeholder**, labeled "Click to add subtitle." To enter text in a placeholder, click the placeholder and then type your text. After you enter text in a placeholder, the placeholder becomes a text object. An **object** is any item on a slide that can be modified. Objects are the building blocks that make up a presentation slide. 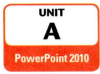 Begin working on your presentation by entering text on the title slide.

STEPS

1. **Move the pointer over the title placeholder labeled Click to add title in the Slide pane**

   The pointer changes to I when you move the pointer over the placeholder. In PowerPoint, the pointer often changes shape, depending on the task you are trying to accomplish.

2. **Click the title placeholder in the Slide pane**

   The **insertion point**, a blinking vertical line, indicates where your text appears when you type in the placeholder. A **selection box** with a dashed line border and **sizing handles** appears around the placeholder, indicating that it is selected and ready to accept text. When a placeholder or object is selected, you can change its shape or size by dragging one of the sizing handles. See Figure A-5.

   TROUBLE
   If you press a wrong key, press [Backspace] to erase the character.

3. **Type Special Summer Adventure Tour Series**

   PowerPoint wraps and then center-aligns the title text within the title placeholder, which is now a text object. Notice that the text also appears on the slide thumbnail on the Slides tab.

4. **Click the subtitle text placeholder in the Slide pane**

   The subtitle text placeholder is ready to accept text.

5. **Type Canadian Train Tours, then press [Enter]**

   The insertion point moves to the next line in the text object.

6. **Type Quest Specialty Travel, press [Enter], type Adventure Tour Series, press [Enter], then type your name**

   Notice that the AutoFit Options button ⊞ appears near the text object. The AutoFit Options button on your screen indicates that PowerPoint has automatically decreased the size of all the text in the text object so that it fits inside the text object.

7. **Click the AutoFit Options button ⊞, then click Stop Fitting Text to This Placeholder on the shortcut menu**

   The text in the text object changes back to its original size and no longer fits in the text object.

8. **In the subtitle text object, position I to the right of Series, drag left to select the entire line of text, press [Backspace], then click outside the text object in a blank area of the slide**

   The Adventure Tour Series line of text is deleted and the AutoFit Options button closes, as shown in Figure A-6. Clicking a blank area of the slide deselects all selected objects on the slide.

9. **Click the Save button 🖫 on the Quick Access toolbar to open the Save As dialog box, then save the presentation as PPT A-QST in the drive and folder where you store your Data Files**

   Notice that PowerPoint automatically enters the title of the presentation as the filename in the Save As dialog box.

FIGURE A-5: Title text placeholder ready to accept text

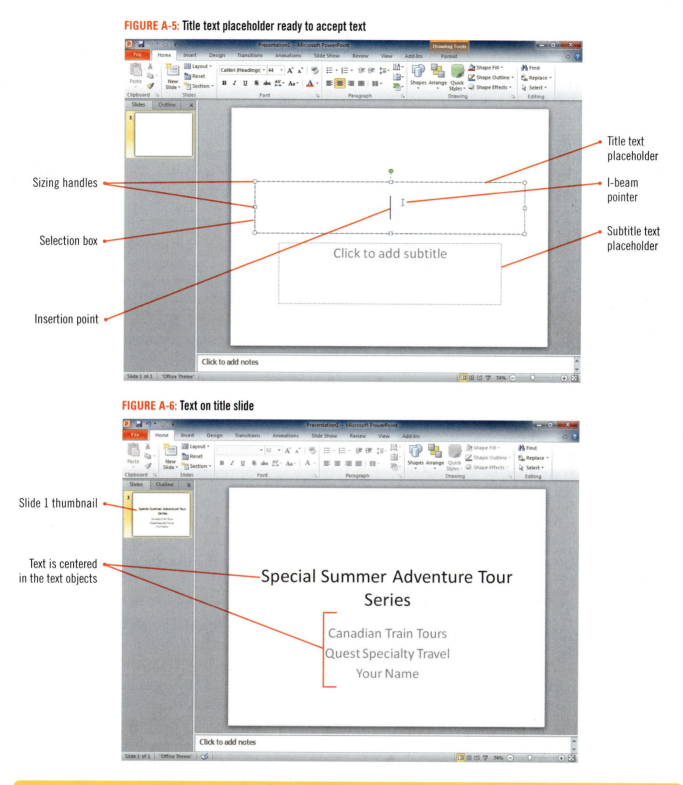

Title text placeholder

I-beam pointer

Subtitle text placeholder

Sizing handles

Selection box

Insertion point

FIGURE A-6: Text on title slide

Slide 1 thumbnail

Text is centered in the text objects

Special Summer Adventure Tour Series

Canadian Train Tours
Quest Specialty Travel
Your Name

Saving fonts with your presentation

When you create a presentation, it uses the fonts that are installed on your computer. If you need to open the presentation on another computer, the fonts might look different if that computer has a different set of fonts. To preserve the look of your presentation on any computer, you can save, or embed, the fonts in your presentation. Click the File tab, then click the Options button. The PowerPoint Options dialog box opens. Click Save in the left pane, then click the Embed fonts in the file check box. Click the Embed all characters option button, then click OK to close the dialog box. Click Save on the Quick Access toolbar. Now the presentation looks the same on any computer that opens it. Using this option, however, significantly increases the size of your presentation, so only use it when necessary. You can freely embed any TrueType or OpenType font that comes with Windows. You can embed other TrueType fonts only if they have no license restrictions.

Adding a New Slide

Ordinarily when you add a new slide to a presentation, you have a pretty good idea of what you want the slide to look like. For example, you may want to add a slide that has a title over bulleted text and a picture. To help you add a slide like this quickly and easily, PowerPoint provides nine standard slide layouts. A **slide layout** contains text and object placeholders that are arranged in a specific way on the slide. You have already worked with the Title Slide layout in the previous lesson. In the event that a standard slide layout does not meet your needs, you can modify an existing slide layout or create a new, custom slide layout. To continue developing the presentation, you create a slide that defines the new tour series.

QUICK TIP
You can easily change the slide layout of the current slide by clicking the Layout button in the Slides group.

1. **Click the New Slide button in the Slides group on the Home tab on the Ribbon**
   A new blank slide (now the current slide) appears as the second slide in your presentation, as shown in Figure A-7. The new slide contains a title placeholder and a content placeholder. A **content placeholder** can be used to insert text or objects such as tables, charts, or pictures. Table A-2 describes the content placeholder icons. Notice that the status bar indicates Slide 2 of 2 and that the Slides tab now contains two slide thumbnails.

2. **Type British Columbia Rail Travel, then click the bottom content placeholder**
   The text you type appears in the title placeholder and the insertion point appears at the top of the bottom content placeholder.

3. **Type Unforgettable scenic views, then press [Enter]**
   The insertion point appears directly below the text when you press [Enter] and a new first-level bullet automatically appears.

4. **Press [Tab]**
   The new first-level bullet is indented and becomes a second-level bullet.

QUICK TIP
You can also press [Shift][Tab] to decrease the indent level.

5. **Type Continental Divide, press [Enter], then click the Decrease List Level button 📑 in the Paragraph group**
   The Decrease List Level button changes the second-level bullet into a first-level bullet.

6. **Type Retrace the steps of historical explorers, then click the New Slide list arrow in the Slides group**
   The Office Theme layout gallery opens. Each slide layout is identified by a descriptive name.

7. **Click the Content with Caption slide layout, then type Beautiful British Columbia**
   A new slide with three content placeholders appears as the third slide.

8. **Click the lower-left placeholder, type Wolf Creek Bridge, press [Enter], click the Increase List Level button 📑, then type Established in 1857 by Fraser Ironworks**
   The Increase List Level button moves the insertion point to the right one level. Notice this text placeholder does not use text bullets to identify separate lines of text.

9. **Click a blank area of the slide, then click the Save button 🖫 on the Quick Access toolbar**
   The Save button saves all of the changes to the file. Compare your screen with Figure A-8.

FIGURE A-7: New blank slide in Normal view

New Slide button

New Slide list arrow

New slide thumbnail added to Slides tab

Total number of slides

Current slide number

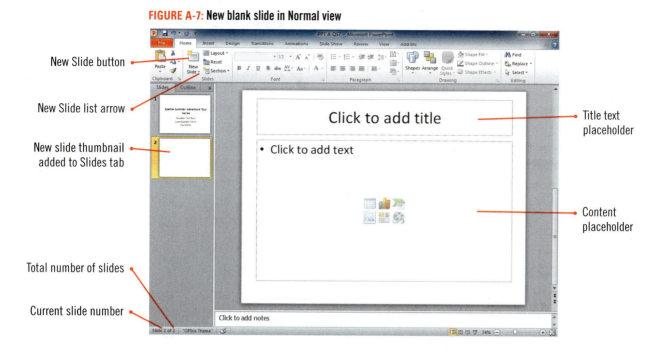

Title text placeholder

Content placeholder

FIGURE A-8: New slide with Content with Caption slide layout

First-level bullet

Second-level bullet

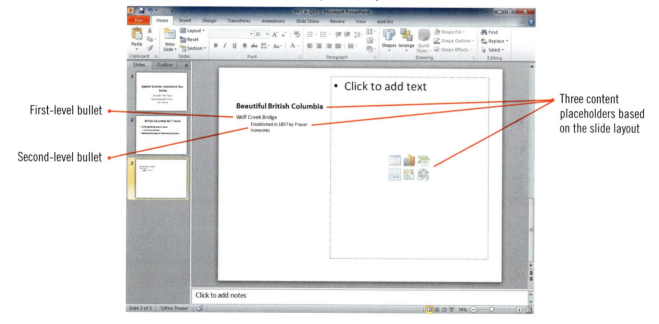

Three content placeholders based on the slide layout

TABLE A-2: Content placeholder icons

click this icon	to insert a
	Table
	Graph chart
	SmartArt graphic
	Picture from a file
	Piece of clip art
	Video clip

Applying a Design Theme

PowerPoint provides a number of design themes to help you quickly create a professional and contemporary looking presentation. A design **theme** includes a set of 12 coordinated colors for fill, line, and shadow, called **theme colors**; a set of fonts for titles and other text, called **theme fonts**; and a set of effects for lines and fills, called **theme effects** to create a cohesive look. In most cases, you would apply one theme to an entire presentation; you can, however, apply multiple themes to the same presentation, or even a different theme on each presentation slide. You can use a design theme as is, or you can alter individual elements of the theme as needed. Unless you need to use a specific design theme, such as a company theme or product design theme, it is faster and easier to use one of the themes supplied with PowerPoint. If you design a custom theme, you can save it to use in the future. 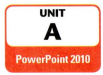 You decide to change the default design theme in the presentation to a new one.

STEPS

1. **Click the Slide 1 thumbnail on the Slides tab**
   Slide 1, the title slide, appears in the Slide pane.

2. **Click the Design tab on the Ribbon, then point to the Adjacency theme in the Themes group as shown in Figure A-9**
   The Design tab appears and a Live Preview of the Adjacency theme is displayed on the slide. A **Live Preview** allows you to see how your changes affect the slides before actually making the change. The Live Preview lasts about 1 minute and then your slide reverts back to its original state. The first (far left) theme thumbnail identifies the current theme applied to the presentation, in this case, the default design theme called the Office Theme. Depending on your monitor resolution and screen size, you can see between five and eleven design themes visible in the Themes group.

3. **Slowly move your pointer ⌖ over the other design themes, then click the Themes group down scroll arrow once**
   A Live Preview of the theme appears on the slide each time you pass your pointer over the theme thumbnails, and a ScreenTip identifies the theme names.

4. **Move ⌖ over the design themes, then click the Couture theme**
   The Couture design theme is applied to all the slides in the presentation. Notice the new slide background color, graphic elements, fonts, and text color. You decide that this theme isn't right for this presentation.

5. **Click the More button ⋮ in the Themes group**
   The All Themes gallery window opens. At the top of the gallery window in the This Presentation section is the current theme applied to the presentation. Notice that just the Couture theme is listed here because when you changed the theme in the last step, you replaced the default theme with the Couture theme. The Built-In section identifies all 40 of the standard themes that come with PowerPoint.

6. **Right-click the Angles theme in the Built-In section, then click Apply to Selected Slides**
   The Angles theme is applied only to Slide 1. You like the Angles theme better and decide to apply it to all slides.

7. **Right-click the Angles theme in the Themes group, then click Apply to All Slides**
   The Angles theme is applied to all three slides. Preview the next slides in the presentation to see how it looks.

8. **Click the Next Slide button ⯆ at the bottom of the vertical scroll bar**
   Compare your screen to Figure A-10.

9. **Click the Previous Slide button ⯅ at the bottom of the vertical scroll bar, then save your changes**

FIGURE A-9: Slide showing a different design theme

Current theme applied

Office theme

Adjacency theme

Themes group down scroll arrow

More button

New font type

New graphic elements

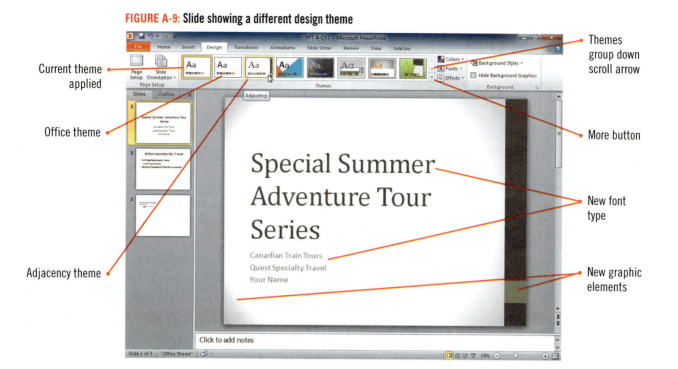

FIGURE A-10: Presentation with Angles theme applied

Angles theme applied to all three slides

Previous Slide button

Next Slide button

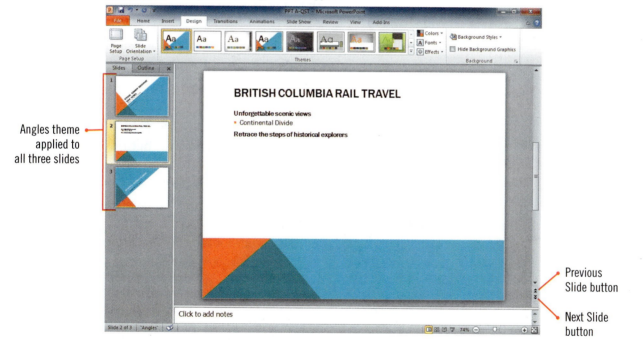

Customizing themes

You are not limited to using the standard themes PowerPoint provides; you can also modify a theme to create your own custom theme. For example, you might want to incorporate your school's or company's colors on the slide background of the presentation or be able to type using fonts your company uses for brand recognition. To modify an existing theme, you can change the color theme, font theme, or the effects theme and then save it for future use by clicking the More button in the Themes group, then clicking Save Current Theme. You also have the ability to create a new font theme or a new color theme from scratch by clicking the Theme Fonts button or the Theme Colors button and then clicking Create New Theme Fonts or Create New Theme Colors. You work in the Create New Theme Fonts or Create New Theme Colors dialog box to define the custom theme fonts or colors.

Comparing Presentation Views

PowerPoint has five primary views: Normal view, Slide Sorter view, Notes Page view, Slide Show view, and Reading view. Each PowerPoint view displays your presentation in a different way and is used for different purposes. Normal view is the primary editing view where you add text, graphics, and other elements to the slides. Slide Sorter view is primarily used to rearrange slides; however, you can also add slide effects and design themes in this view. You use Notes Page view to type notes that are important for each slide. Slide Show view displays your presentation over the whole computer screen and is designed to show your presentation to an audience. Similar to Slide Show view, Reading view is designed to view your presentation on a computer screen. To move easily among the main PowerPoint views, use the View Shortcuts buttons located on the Status bar next to the Zoom slider. Most PowerPoint views can be accessed using the View tab on the Ribbon. Table A-3 provides a brief description of the PowerPoint views. Examine each of the PowerPoint views, starting with Normal view.

STEPS

1. **Click the Outline tab, then click the small slide icon ▦ next to Slide 2 in the Outline tab**

   The text for Slide 2 is selected in the Outline tab, and Slide 2 appears in the Slide pane, as shown in Figure A-11. Notice that the status bar identifies the number of the slide you are viewing, the total number of slides in the presentation, and the name of the applied design theme.

2. **Click the Slides tab, then click the Slide 1 thumbnail**

   Slide 1 appears in the Slide pane. Thumbnails of the slides in your presentation appear again on the Slides tab. Since the Slides tab is by default narrower than the Outline tab, the Slide pane enlarges. The scroll box in the vertical scroll bar moves back up the scroll bar.

   > **QUICK TIP**
   > You can also switch between views using the commands in the Presentation Views group on the View tab.

3. **Click the Slide Sorter button ▦ on the status bar**

   A thumbnail of each slide in the presentation appears in the window. You can examine the flow of your slides and drag any slide or group of slides to rearrange the order of the slides in the presentation.

4. **Double-click the Slide 1 thumbnail, then click the Reading View button ▦ on the status bar**

   The first slide fills the screen as shown in Figure A-12. Use Reading view to review your presentation or to show your presentation to someone directly on your computer. The status bar controls at the bottom of the window make it easy to move between slides in this view.

5. **Click the Slide Show button ▦ on the status bar**

   The first slide fills the entire screen now without the title bar and status bar. In this view, you can practice running through your slides as they would appear in a slide show.

   > **QUICK TIP**
   > You can also press [Enter], [Spacebar], [Page Up], [Page Down], or the arrow keys to advance the slide show.

6. **Click the left mouse button to advance through the slides one at a time until you see a black slide, then click once more to return to Normal view**

   The black slide at the end of the slide show indicates that the slide show is finished. At the end of a slide show you automatically return to the slide and PowerPoint view you were in before you ran the slide show, in this case Slide 1 in Normal view.

7. **Click the View tab on the Ribbon, then click the Notes Page button in the Presentation Views group**

   Notes Page view appears, showing a reduced image of the current slide above a large text placeholder. You can enter text in this placeholder and then print the notes page for your own use.

8. **Click the Normal button in the Presentation Views group**

FIGURE A-11: Normal view with the outline tab displayed

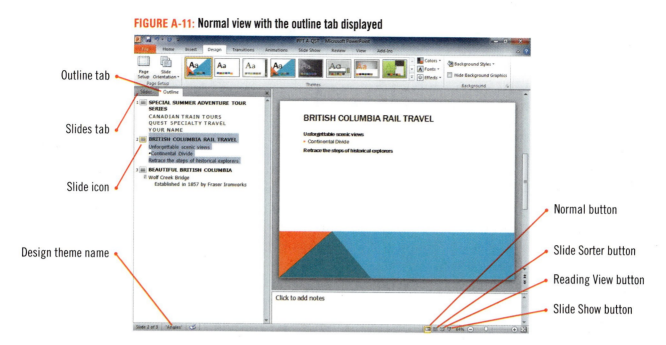

- Outline tab
- Slides tab
- Slide icon
- Design theme name
- Normal button
- Slide Sorter button
- Reading View button
- Slide Show button

FIGURE A-12: Reading view

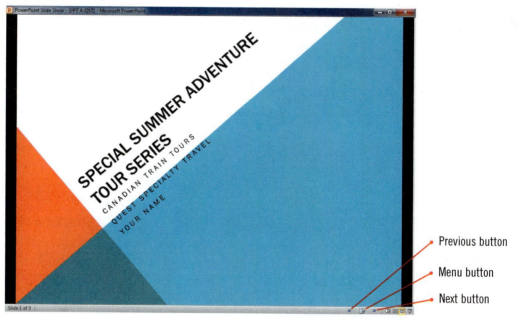

- Previous button
- Menu button
- Next button

TABLE A-3: PowerPoint views

view name	button	button name	description
Normal		Normal	Displays the Outline and Slides tabs, the Slide pane, and the Notes pane at the same time; use this view to work on your presentation's content, layout, and notes concurrently
Slide Sorter		Slide Sorter	Displays thumbnails of all slides; use this view to rearrange and add special effects to your slides
Slide Show		Slide Show	Displays your presentation on the whole computer screen
Reading View		Reading View	Displays your presentation in a large window on your computer screen
Notes Page	(no View Shortcuts button)		Displays a reduced image of the current slide above a large text box where you can enter or view notes

Printing a PowerPoint Presentation

You print your presentation when you want to review your work or when you have completed it and want a hard copy. Reviewing your presentation at different stages of development gives you a better perspective of the overall flow and feel of the presentation. You can also preview your presentation to see exactly how each slide looks before you print the presentation. When you are finished working on your presentation, even if it is not yet complete, you can close the presentation file and exit PowerPoint. You are done working on the tour presentation for now. You save and preview the presentation, then you print the slides and notes pages of the presentation so you can review them later. Before leaving for the day, you close the file and exit PowerPoint.

STEPS

1. **Click the Save button 🖫 on the Quick Access toolbar, click the File tab on the Ribbon, then click Print**

   The Print window opens as shown in Figure A-13. Notice the preview pane on the right side of the window that automatically displays the first slide of the presentation.

   QUICK TIP
   To quickly print the presentation with the current Print options, add the Quick Print button to the Quick Access toolbar.

2. **Click the Next Page button ▶ at the bottom of the preview pane, then click ▶ again**

   Each slide in the presentation appears in the preview pane.

3. **Click the Print button**

   Each slide in the presentation prints.

4. **Click the File tab on the Ribbon, click Print, then click the Full Page Slides button in the Settings section**

   The Print Layout gallery opens. In this gallery you can specify what you want to print (slides, handouts, notes pages, or outline), as well as other print options. To save paper when you are reviewing your slides, you can print in handout format, which lets you print up to nine slides per page. The options you choose in the Print window remain there until you change them or close the presentation.

   QUICK TIP
   To print slides appropriate in size for overhead transparencies, click the Design tab, click the Page Setup button in the Page Setup group, click the Slides sized for list arrow, then click Overhead.

5. **Click 3 Slides, click the Color button in the Settings section, then click Pure Black and White**

   PowerPoint removes the color and displays the slides as thumbnails next to blank lines as shown in Figure A-14. Using the Handouts with three slides per page printing option is a great way to print your presentation when you want to provide a way for audience members to take notes. Printing pure black-and-white prints without any gray tones can save printer toner.

6. **Click the Print button**

   The presentation prints one page showing the all the slides of the presentation as thumbnails next to blank lines.

7. **Click the File tab on the Ribbon, then click Close**

   If you have made changes to your presentation, a Microsoft PowerPoint alert box opens asking you if you want to save changes you have made to your presentation file.

8. **Click Save, if necessary, to close the alert box**

   Your presentation closes.

9. **Click the File tab on the Ribbon, then click Exit**

   The PowerPoint program closes, and you return to the Windows desktop.

FIGURE A-13: Print window

Current printer

Current print settings

Click to change the print range

Click to select a print layout

Previous button

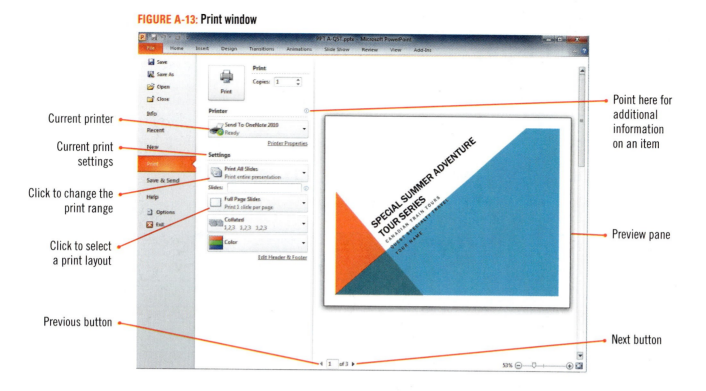

Point here for additional information on an item

Preview pane

Next button

FIGURE A-14: Print window with changed settings

Print button

Your printer name may be different

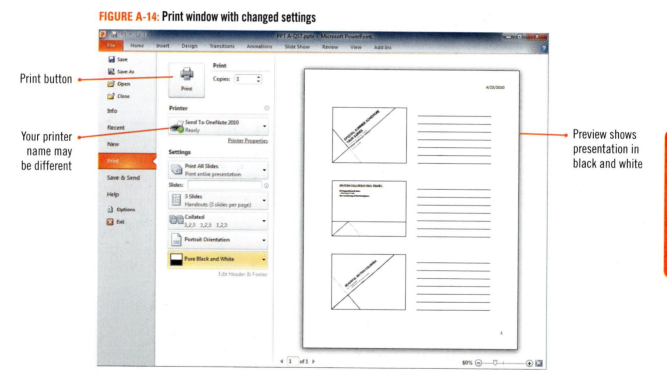

Preview shows presentation in black and white

Windows Live and Microsoft Office Web Apps

All Office programs include the capability to incorporate feedback—called online collaboration—across the Internet or a company network. Using **cloud computing** (work done in a virtual environment), you can take advantage of Web programs called Microsoft Office Web Apps, which are simplified versions of the programs found in the Microsoft Office 2010 suite. Because these programs are online, they take up no computer disk space and are accessed using Windows Live

SkyDrive, a free service from Microsoft. Using Windows Live SkyDrive, you and your colleagues can create and store documents in a "cloud" and make the documents available to whomever you grant access. To use Windows Live SkyDrive, you need a free Windows Live ID, which you obtain at the Windows Live Web site. You can find more information in the "Working with Windows Live and Microsoft Office Web Apps" appendix.

Practice

Concepts Review

For current SAM information, including versions and content details, visit SAM Central (http://www.cengage.com/samcentral). If you have a SAM user profile, you may have access to hands-on instruction, practice, and assessment of the skills covered in this unit. Since various versions of SAM are supported throughout the life of this text, check with your instructor for the correct instructions and URL/Web site for accessing assignments.

Label each element of the PowerPoint window shown in Figure A-15.

FIGURE A-15

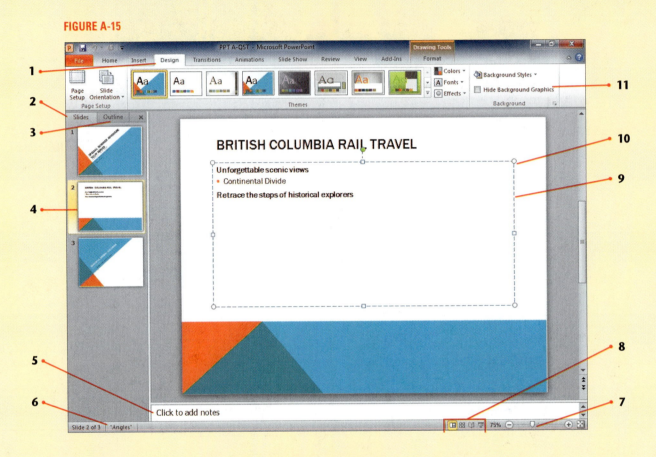

Match each term with the statement that best describes it.

12. Reading view
13. Notes pane
14. Slide Show view
15. Slide Layout
16. Ribbon
17. Zoom slider

a. A view that displays a presentation over an entire computer screen and that is used to show to an audience

b. Allows you to change the size of the slide in the window

c. A view that is used to review a presentation or to show someone a presentation directly on a computer screen

d. Arranges placeholders in a specific way on the slide

e. Used to type text that references slide content

f. Used to organize all of the commands in PowerPoint

Select the best answer from the list of choices.

18. Which statement about incorporating information is *not* correct?

a. You can import text and numerical data into PowerPoint.

b. You can open a PowerPoint presentation in another program to incorporate data.

c. Images from Adobe Photoshop can be inserted into a presentation.

d. Graphic images from a digital camera can be inserted into PowerPoint.

19. Finish the following sentence: "Copyright protects the expression of an idea,...":

a. But not the underlying facts or concepts.

b. Including all general subject matter.

c. Only if you have it regestered with the Copyright Office.

d. Under the Fair Use policy.

20. Which of the following is/are located on the status bar and allow you to quickly switch between views?

a. Fit slide to current window button

b. Switch view button

c. Zoom Slider

d. View Shortcuts

21. What is the blinking vertical line that appears when you type text called?

a. Text handle

b. Placeholder

c. Text insertion line

d. Insertion point

22. The view that fills the entire screen with each slide in the presentation without the title bar is called:

a. Slide Show view.

b. Fit to window view.

c. Reading view.

d. Normal view.

23. Other than the Slide pane, where else can you enter slide text?

a. Reading pane

b. Notes Page view

c. Outline tab

d. Slides tab

24. What does the slide layout do in a presentation?

a. The slide layout puts all your slides in order.

b. A slide layout automatically applies all the objects you can use on a slide.

c. A slide layout defines how all the elements on a slide are arranged.

d. The slide layout enables you to apply a template to the presentation.

25. Which of the following is not included in a design theme?

a. Effects

b. Pictures

c. Colors

d. Fonts

Skills Review

1. Examine the PowerPoint window.

a. Start PowerPoint, if necessary.

b. Identify as many elements of the PowerPoint window as you can without referring to the unit material.

c. Be able to describe the purpose or function of each element.

d. For any elements you cannot identify, refer to the unit.

2. Enter slide text.

a. In the Slide pane in Normal view, enter the text **Alutiiq Indian Lands Protection Proposal** in the title placeholder. Refer to Figure A-16 as you complete the slide.

b. In the subtitle text placeholder, enter **Karluk Lake on Kodiak Island**.

FIGURE A-16

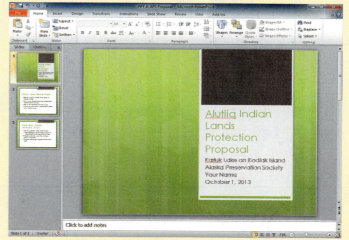

Skills Review (continued)

   c. On the next line of the placeholder, enter **Alaska Preservation Society**.

   d. On the next line of the placeholder, enter your name.

   e. On the next line of the placeholder, enter **October 1, 2013**. Let PowerPoint AutoFit the text in the text object.

   f. Deselect the text object.

   g. Save the presentation using the filename **PPT A-APS Proposal** to the drive and folder where you store your Data Files.

3. Add a new slide.

   a. Create a new slide.

   b. Using Figure A-17, enter text on the slide.

   c. Create another new slide.

   d. Using Figure A-18, enter text on the slide.

   e. Save your changes.

4. Apply a design theme.

   a. Click the Design tab.

   b. Click the Themes group More button, then point to all of the themes.

   c. Locate the Grid theme, then apply it to the selected slide.

   d. Move to Slide 1.

   e. Locate the Austin theme, then apply it to Slide 1.

   f. Apply the Austin theme to all of the slides in the presentation.

   g. Use the Next Slide button to move to Slide 3, then save your changes.

5. Compare presentation views.

   a. Click the View tab.

   b. Click the Slide Sorter button in the Presentation Views group.

   c. Click the Notes Page button in the Presentation Views group, then click the Previous Slide button twice.

   d. Click the Reading View button in the Presentation Views group, then click the Next button on the status bar.

   e. Click the Normal button on the status bar, then click the Slide Show button.

   f. Advance the slides until a black screen appears, then click to end the presentation.

   g. Save your changes.

6. Print a presentation.

   a. Print all the slides as handouts, 4 Slides Horizontal, in color.

   b. Print the presentation outline.

   c. Close the file, saving your changes.

   d. Exit PowerPoint.

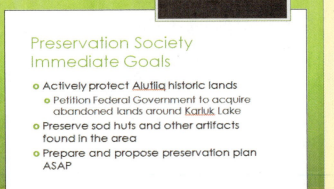

FIGURE A-17

Karluk Lake Historic Facts

- Covers over 170 acres in the heart of Kodiak Island
- First Alutiiq Indian settlement established before the 8th century
- Key winter settlement for the Alutiiq
- Numerous sod houses and artifacts found within last 10 years

FIGURE A-18

Preservation Society Immediate Goals

- Actively protect Alutiiq historic lands
  - Petition Federal Government to acquire abandoned lands around Karluk Lake
- Preserve sod huts and other artifacts found in the area
- Prepare and propose preservation plan ASAP

Independent Challenge 1

You work for BioCare Service Industries, a business that offers environmental hazard cleanup and project management. One of your jobs at the company is to go on new sales calls with your boss. Your boss has asked you to create a sales presentation that describes and compares the services BioCare Industries offers.

If you have a SAM 2010 user profile, an autogradable SAM version of this assignment may be available at http://www.cengage.com/sam2010. Check with your instructor to confirm that this assignment is available in SAM. To use the SAM version of this assignment, log into the SAM 2010 Web site and download the instruction and start files.

a. Start PowerPoint.

b. In the title placeholder on Slide 1, type **BioCare Service Industries**.

c. In the subtitle placeholder, type your name, press [Enter], then type today's date.

d. Apply the Thatch design theme to the presentation.

e. Save your presentation with the filename **PPT A-BioCare** to the drive and folder where you store your Data Files.

f. Use Figures A-19 and A-20 to add two more slides to your presentation. (*Hint*: Slide 2 uses the Comparison layout.)

g. Use the commands on the View tab to switch between all of PowerPoint's views.

h. Print the presentation using handouts, 3 Slides, in black and white.

i. Save and close the file, then exit PowerPoint.

FIGURE A-19

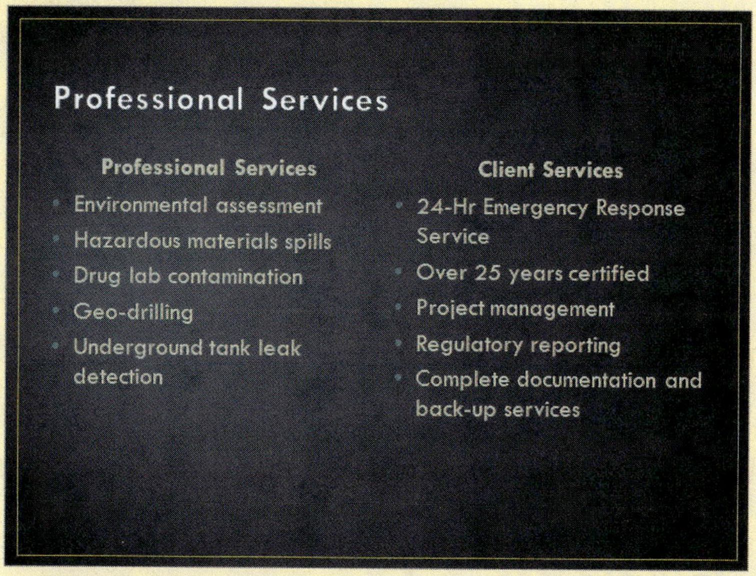

Professional Services

Professional Services	Client Services
• Environmental assessment	• 24-Hr Emergency Response Service
• Hazardous materials spills	• Over 25 years certified
• Drug lab contamination	• Project management
• Geo-drilling	• Regulatory reporting
• Underground tank leak detection	• Complete documentation and back-up services

FIGURE A-20

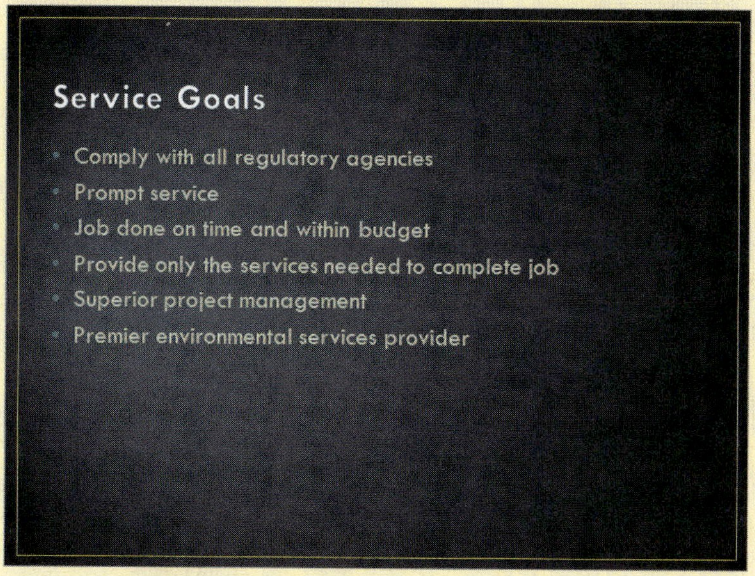

Service Goals

- Comply with all regulatory agencies
- Prompt service
- Job done on time and within budget
- Provide only the services needed to complete job
- Superior project management
- Premier environmental services provider

Independent Challenge 2

You have recently been promoted to sales manager at PowerCraft Sports, which manufactures personal aircraft, including different types of ultralite and composite airplanes. Part of your job is to present company sales figures at a yearly sales meeting. Use the following information as the basis for units sold nationally in your presentation: 283 Aircruiser, 105 Aero Twin, 89 UltraFlight, 73 Tomahawk V, and 47 Vision II. Assume that PowerCraft Sports has six sales regions throughout the country: Northwest, West, South, Midwest, Mid Atlantic, and Northeast. Also, assume overall sales rose 5% over last year, and gross sales reached $49 million. The presentation should have at least five slides.

a. Spend some time planning the slides of your presentation. What is the best way to show the information provided? What other information could you add that might be useful for this presentation?

b. Start PowerPoint.

c. Give the presentation an appropriate title on the title slide, and enter today's date and your name in the subtitle placeholder.

d. Add slides and enter appropriate slide text.

e. On the last slide of the presentation, include the following information:

PowerCraft Sports

PO Box 7373

Wrightsville, NC 19698-7373

f. Apply a design theme. A typical slide might look like the one shown in Figure A-21.

FIGURE A-21

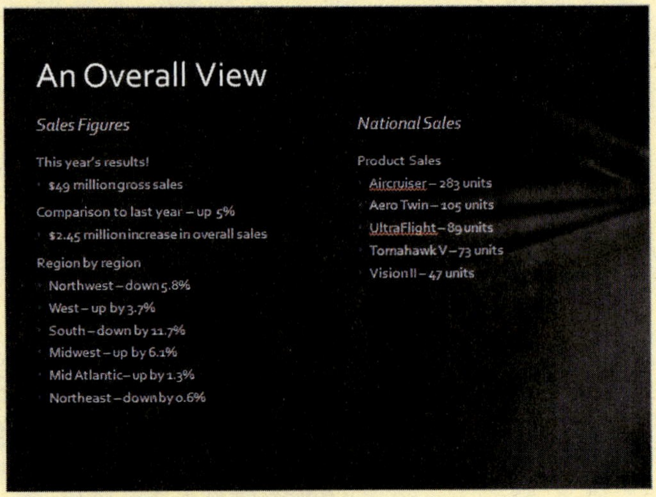

An Overall View

Sales Figures

This year's results!
- $49 million gross sales

Comparison to last year – up 5%
- $2.45 million increase in overall sales

Region by region
- Northwest – down 5.8%
- West – up by 3.7%
- South – down by 11.7%
- Midwest – up by 6.1%
- Mid Atlantic – up by 1.3%
- Northeast – down by 0.6%

National Sales

Product Sales
- Aircruiser – 283 units
- Aero Twin – 105 units
- UltraFlight – 89 units
- Tomahawk V – 73 units
- Vision II – 47 units

Advanced Challenge Exercise

- Open the Notes Page view.
- Add notes to three slides.
- Print the Notes Page view for the presentation.

g. Switch views. Run through the slide show at least once.

h. Save your presentation with the filename **PPT A-PowerCraft Sports** where you store your Data Files.

i. Close the presentation and exit PowerPoint.

Independent Challenge 3

You work for Baja Central, an emerging company that exports goods from Mexico. The company wants to expand its business globally. The Internet marketing director has asked you to plan and create a PowerPoint presentation that he will use to convey an expanded Internet service that will target Western countries. This new Internet service will allow customers to purchase all kinds of Mexican-made goods. Sample items for sale include silver and turquoise jewelry, hand crafts, folk art, terra cotta kitchenware, wood decorative items, and leather goods. Your presentation should contain product information and pricing. Use the Internet, if possible, to research information that will help you formulate your ideas. The presentation should have at least five slides.

a. Spend some time planning the slides of your presentation. What information would a consumer need to have to purchase items on this Web site?

b. Start PowerPoint.

c. Give the presentation an appropriate title on the title slide, and enter today's date and your name in the subtitle placeholder.

d. Add slides and enter appropriate slide text.

Independent Challenge 3 (continued)

e. On the last slide of the presentation, type the following information:

Baja Central Ltd.

Adolfo P Limon "T"

Oaxaca, Oax

ZC 98000

Tel: 50-001-660-44

info@bjacenltd.com

f. Apply a design theme. A typical slide might look like the one shown in Figure A-22.

g. Switch views. Run through the slide show at least once.

h. Save your presentation with the filename **PPT A-Baja** where you store your Data Files.

i. Close the presentation and exit PowerPoint.

FIGURE A-22

FINE JEWELRY PRODUCT LIST

Silver Jewelry	Turquoise Jewelry
• Bracelets	• Bracelets
• Earrings	• Earrings
• Necklaces	• Necklaces
• Pendants	• Rings
• Rings	
• Watches	

Real Life Independent Challenge

Every year your college holds a large fund-raising event to support a local charity. You are a member of the Student Council Advisory Board (SCAB), which is in charge of deciding which charity gets help. This year the board decided to support the city food bank by hosting a chili cook-off competition. The competition needs to include local and professional cooking teams from around the region. You have been chosen to present the charity proposal in a meeting of the College Events Council.

a. Spend some time planning the slides of your presentation. Assume the following: the competition is a 2-day event; event advertising will be city- and regionwide; local music groups will also be invited; there will be a kids section with events and games; the event will be held at the county fairgrounds. Use the Internet, if possible, to research information that will help you formulate your ideas.

b. Start PowerPoint.

c. Give the presentation an appropriate title on the title slide and enter your school's name, your name, and today's date in the subtitle placeholder.

d. Add slides and enter appropriate slide text. You must create at least three slides. Typical slides might look like the ones shown in Figure A-23 and Figure A-24.

e. View the presentation.

f. Save your presentation with the filename **PPT A-Chili Cookoff** where you store your Data Files.

g. Close the presentation and exit PowerPoint.

FIGURE A-23

Planning Committee

☙ Form working committee
 ☙ Set up budget
  ☙ Get approval
☙ Arrange facilities, entertainment, etc.
 ☙ County Fairgrounds
 ☙ Kids games and events
 ☙ Local bands
☙ Invite local and regional professional teams
☙ Solicit local businesses for cash and other prizes
 ☙ Advertising/marketing

FIGURE A-24

Judging Schedule

Saturday – Prelims	Sunday – Finals
☙ 2:30pm – Chili	☙ 11:00 am – Dessert
☙ 4:15pm – Chili with meat	☙ 11:30am – Side Dish
☙ 5:30pm – Side Dishes	☙ 12:00am – Chili
☙ 7:00pm – Desserts	☙ 12:30am – Chili with meat
	☙ 1:00pm – Winner's Cook-off Dinner

Visual Workshop

Create the presentation shown in Figures A-25 and A-26. Make sure you include your name on the title slide. Save the presentation as **PPT A-Landscape Industries** where you store your Data Files. Print the slides.

FIGURE A-25

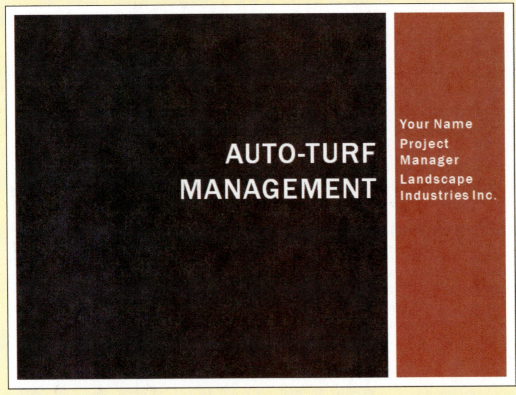

FIGURE A-26

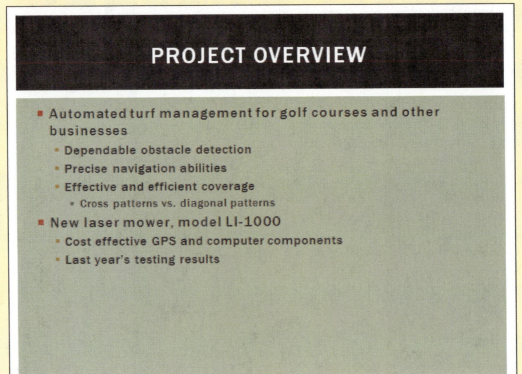

Modifying a Presentation

Files You Will Need:

PPT B-1.pptx
PPT B-2.pptx
PPT B-3.pptx
PPT B-4.pptx
PPT B-5.pptx

In the previous unit you learned how to enter slide text, add a new slide, and apply a design theme. Now, you are ready to take the next step in creating professional-looking presentations by learning to format text and work with drawn objects. In this unit, you'll enter text in the Outline tab, format text, draw and modify objects, add slide footer information, and check the spelling in the presentation. You continue working on your Canadian Train tour presentation.

OBJECTIVES

Enter text in the Outline tab

Format text

Convert text to SmartArt

Insert and modify shapes

Edit and duplicate shapes

Align and group objects

Add slide headers and footers

Use proofing and language tools

Entering Text in the Outline Tab

You can enter presentation text by typing directly on the slide in the Slide pane, or, if you'd rather focus on the presentation text without worrying about the layout, you can enter text in the Outline tab. The outline is organized so that the headings, or slide titles, appear at the top of the outline. Beneath the title, each subpoint, or each line of bulleted text, appears as one or more indented lines under the title. Each indent in the outline creates another level of bulleted text on the slide.  You switch to the Outline tab to enter text for two more slides for your presentation.

STEPS

QUICK TIP
To open a PowerPoint 97-2003 presentation in PowerPoint 2010, open the presentation, click the File tab, click the Convert button, name the presentation file in the Save As dialog box, then click Save.

1. **Start PowerPoint, open the presentation PPT B-1.pptx from the drive and folder where you store your Data Files, then save it as PPT B-QST.pptx**
   A presentation with the new name appears in the PowerPoint window.

2. **Click the Slide 2 thumbnail in the Slides tab, then click the Outline tab**
   The Outline tab enlarges to display the text that is on the slides. The slide icon and the text for Slide 2 are highlighted, indicating that it is selected.

3. **On the Home tab on the Ribbon, click the New Slide list arrow in the Slides group, then click Title and Content**
   A new slide, Slide 3, with the Title and Content layout appears as the current slide below Slide 2. A blinking insertion point appears next to the new slide in the Outline tab. Text that you enter next to a slide icon becomes the title for that slide.

4. **Type Canadian Rockies Tours, press [Enter], then press [Tab]**
   When you first press [Enter] you create a new slide, but because you want to enter bulleted text on Slide 3 you press [Tab] so that the text you type is entered as bullet text on Slide 3. See Figure B-1. Notice the text you type is in all uppercase letters because that is how the font is set in the design theme.

5. **Type British Columbia Railways Inc., press [Enter], type Based in Vancouver BC, then press [Enter]**
   Each time you press [Enter], the insertion point moves down one line.

6. **Press [Shift][Tab]**
   Because you are working in the Outline tab, a new slide, Slide 4, is created when you press [Shift][Tab].

QUICK TIP
Press [Ctrl][Enter] while the cursor is in the text object to create a new slide with the same layout as the previous slide.

7. **Type BC Railways Service Packages, press [Ctrl][Enter], type Royal Package, press [Enter], type Exclusve Package, make sure you misspell the word "Exclusve," press [Enter] type Deluxe Package, press [Enter], then type Classic Package**
   Pressing [Ctrl][Enter] while the cursor is in the title text object moves the cursor into the content placeholder.

8. **Position the pointer on the Slide 3 icon in the Outline tab**
   The pointer changes to ✛. Slide 3, Canadian Rockies Tours slide, is out of order.

9. **Drag the Slide 3 icon up until a horizontal indicator line appears above the Slide 2 icon, then release the mouse button**
   The third slide moves up and switches places with the second slide as shown in Figure B-2.

10. **Click the Slides tab, then save your work**
    The Outline tab closes and the Slides tab is now visible in the window.

FIGURE B-1: Outline tab showing new slide

Outline tab

New slide

New slide title

New slide with Title and Content layout

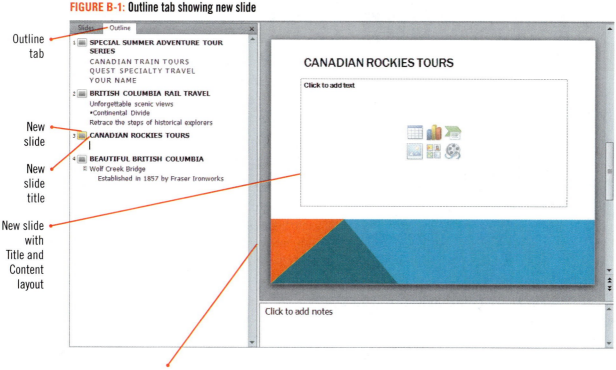

Drag the pane divider to change the width of the Outline tab

FIGURE B-2: Outline tab showing moved slide

Move pointer

Moved slide

Make sure you misspell this word

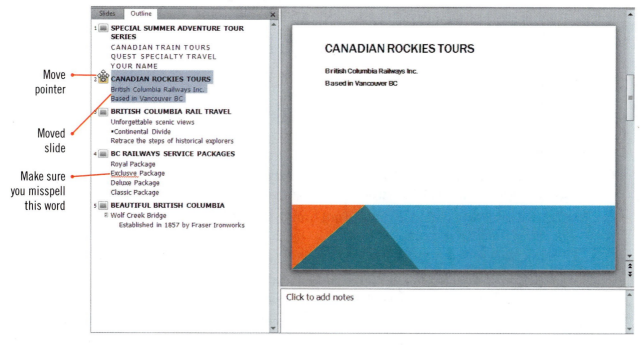

Setting permissions

In PowerPoint, you can set specific access permissions for people who review or edit your work, so you have better control over your content. For example, you may want to give a user permission to edit or change your presentation but not allow them to print it. You can also restrict a user by permitting them to view the presentation, without the ability to edit or print the presentation, or you can give the user full access or control of the presentation. To use this feature, you first have to have access to an Information Rights Management Service from Microsoft or another rights management company. Then, to set user access permissions, click the File tab, click Info, click the Protect Presentation button, point to Restrict Permission by People, then click an appropriate option.

Formatting Text

Once you have entered and edited the text in your presentation, you can modify the way the text looks to emphasize your message. Important text should be highlighted in some way to distinguish it from other text or objects on the slide. For example, if you have two text objects on the same slide, you could draw attention to one text object by changing its color, font, or size.  You decide to format the text on Slide 2 of the presentation.

STEPS

QUICK TIP
To show or hide the Mini toolbar, click the File tab on the Ribbon, then click Options.

1. **Click the Slide 2 thumbnail in the Slides tab, then double-click Canadian in the title text object**

    The word "Canadian" is selected, and a small semitransparent Mini toolbar appears above the text. The **Mini toolbar** contains basic text-formatting commands, such as bold and italic, and appears when you select text using the mouse. This toolbar makes it quick and easy to format text, especially when the Home tab is not open.

2. **Move the pointer over the Mini toolbar, click the Font Color list arrow A ⋅, then click the Purple color box under Standard Colors**

    The text changes color to purple as shown in Figure B-3. As soon as you move the pointer over the Mini toolbar, the toolbar becomes clearly visible. When you click the Font Color list arrow, the Font Color gallery appears showing the Theme Colors and Standard Colors. Notice that the Font Color button on the Mini toolbar and the Font Color button in the Font group on the Home tab change color to reflect the new color choice.

QUICK TIP
To select an unselected text object, press [Shift], click the text object, then release [Shift].

3. **Move the pointer over the title text object border until the pointer changes to ⁘, then click the border**

    The entire title text object is selected, and changes you make now affect all of the text in the text object. When the whole text object is selected, you can change its size, shape, or other attributes. Changing the color of the text helps emphasize it.

4. **Click the Font Color button A ⋅ in the Font group**

    All of the text in the title text object changes to the purple color.

5. **Click the Font list arrow in the Font group**

    A list of available fonts opens with Franklin Gothic Medium, the current font used in the title text object, selected at the top of the list in the Theme Fonts section.

6. **Click Algerian in the All Fonts section**

    The Algerian font replaces the original font in the title text object. Notice that as you move the pointer over the font names in the font list the text on the slide displays a Live Preview of the different font choices.

7. **Click the Underline button U in the Font group, then click the Increase Font Size button A˙ in the Font group**

    All of the text now displays an underline and increases in size to 32.

8. **Click the Character Spacing button AV ⋅ in the Font group, then click Loose**

    The spacing between the letters in the title text box increases slightly. Compare your screen to Figure B-4.

9. **Click a blank area of the slide outside the text object to deselect it, then save your work**

FIGURE B-3: Selected word with Mini toolbar open

FIGURE B-3: Selected word with Mini toolbar open

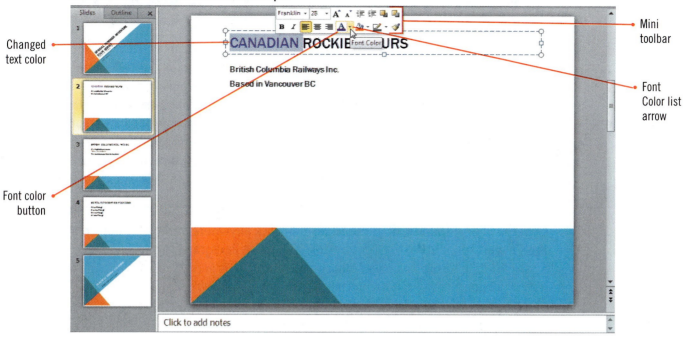

Changed text color

Font color button

Mini toolbar

Font Color list arrow

FIGURE B-4: Formatted text

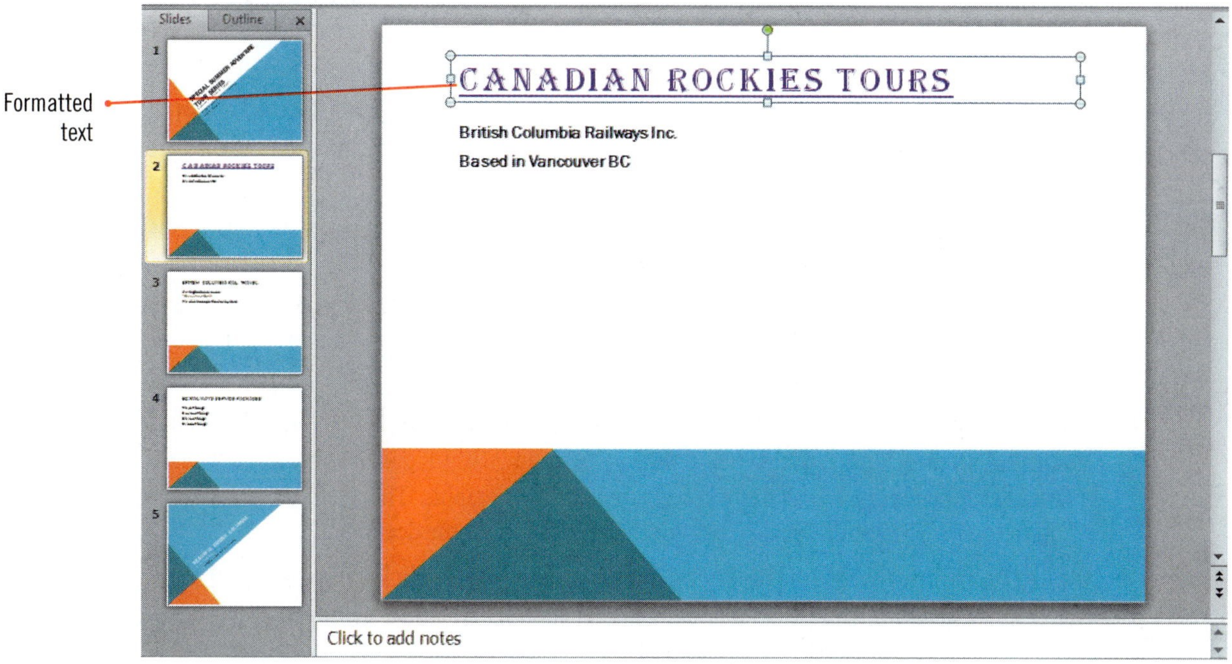

Formatted text

Replacing text and fonts

As you review your presentation, you may decide to replace certain text or fonts throughout the entire presentation using the Replace command. Text can be a word, phrase, or sentence. To replace specific text, click the Home tab on the Ribbon, then click the Replace button in the Editing group. In the Replace dialog box, enter the text you want to replace then enter the text you want to use as its replacement. You can also use the Replace command to replace one font for another. Simply click the Replace button list arrow in the Editing group, then click Replace Fonts to open the Replace Font dialog box.

PowerPoint 2010

Modifying a Presentation

PowerPoint 29

Converting Text to SmartArt

Sometimes when you are working with text it just doesn't capture your attention, no matter how you dress it up with color or other formatting attributes. The ability to convert text to a SmartArt graphic increases your ability to create dynamic-looking text. A **SmartArt** graphic is a professional-quality diagram that visually illustrates text. There are eight categories, or types, of SmartArt graphics that incorporate graphics to illustrate text differently. For example, you can show steps in a process or timeline, show proportional relationships, or show how parts relate to a whole. You can create a SmartArt graphic from scratch or create one by converting existing text you have entered on a slide with a few simple clicks of the mouse. You want the presentation to appear visually dynamic so you convert the text on Slide 4 to a SmartArt graphic.

STEPS

1. **Click the Slide 4 thumbnail in the Slides tab, click anywhere in the text object, then click the Convert to SmartArt Graphic button 🖼️ in the Paragraph group**

    A gallery of SmartArt graphic layouts opens. As with many features in PowerPoint, you can preview how your text will look prior to applying the SmartArt graphic layout by using PowerPoint's Live Preview feature. You can review each SmartArt graphic layout and see how it changes the appearance of text.

2. **Move the pointer over the SmartArt graphic layouts in the gallery**

    Notice how the text becomes part of the graphic and the color and font changes each time you move the pointer over a different graphic layout. SmartArt graphic names appear as ScreenTips.

TROUBLE

If the text pane does not open as shown in Figure B-5, click the Text pane button in the Create Graphic group.

3. **Click the Pyramid List layout in the SmartArt graphics gallery**

    A SmartArt graphic appears on the slide in place of the text object, and a new SmartArt Tools Design tab opens on the Ribbon as shown in Figure B-5. A SmartArt graphic consists of two parts: the SmartArt graphic itself and a Text pane where you type and edit text.

4. **Click each bullet point in the Text pane, then click the Text pane Close button**

    Notice that each time you select a bullet point in the text pane, a selection box appears around the text objects in the SmartArt graphic. The text pane closes.

QUICK TIP

Text objects in the SmartArt graphic can be moved and edited like any other text object in PowerPoint.

5. **Click the More button ▾ in the Layouts group, click More Layouts, click the Basic Matrix layout in the Matrix section, then click OK**

    The SmartArt graphic changes to the new graphic layout. You can radically change how the SmartArt graphic looks by applying a SmartArt Style. A **SmartArt Style** is a preset combination of simple and 3-D formatting options that follows the presentation theme.

6. **Move the pointer slowly over the styles in the SmartArt Styles group, then click the More button ▾ in the SmartArt Styles group**

    A Live Preview of each style is displayed on the SmartArt graphic. The SmartArt styles are organized into sections; the top group offers suggestions for the best match for the document.

QUICK TIP

Click the Convert button in the Reset group then click Convert to Text to revert the SmartArt graphic to a standard text object.

7. **Move the pointer over all the styles in the gallery, then click Intense Effect**

    Notice how the new Intense Effect style adds a bevel and top-left corner lighting to the text boxes.

8. **Click a blank area of the slide outside the SmartArt graphic object to deselect it, then save your work**

    Compare your screen to Figure B-6.

FIGURE B-5: Text converted to a SmartArt graphic

Text pane button

Text pane Close button

Text pane

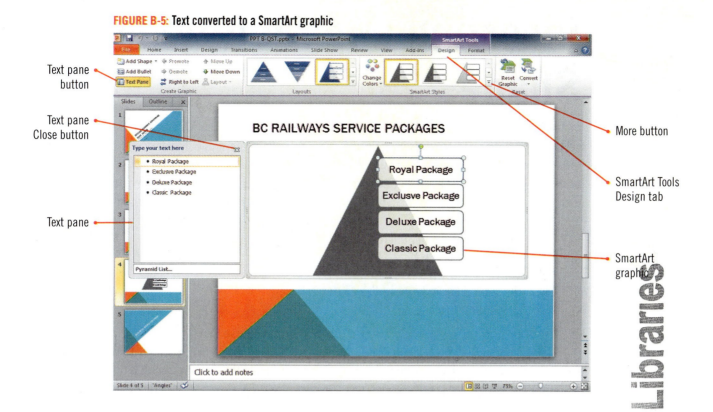

More button

SmartArt Tools Design tab

SmartArt graphic

FIGURE B-6: Final SmartArt graphic

Choosing SmartArt graphics

When choosing a SmartArt graphic to use on your slide, remember that you want the SmartArt graphic to communicate the message of the text effectively; not every SmartArt graphic layout achieves that goal. You must consider the type of text you want to illustrate. For example, does the text show steps in a process, does it show a continual process, or does it show nonsequential information? The answer to this question will dictate the type of SmartArt graphic layout you should choose. Also, the amount of text you want to illustrate will have an effect on the SmartArt graphic layout you choose. Most of the time key points will be the text you use in a SmartArt graphic. Finally, some SmartArt graphic layouts are limited by the number of shapes that they can accommodate, so be sure to choose a graphic layout that can illustrate your text appropriately. Experiment with the SmartArt graphic layouts until you find the right one, and have fun in the process!

Inserting and Modifying Shapes

In PowerPoint you can insert many different types of shapes including lines, geometric figures, arrows, stars, callouts, and banners to enhance your presentation. You can create single shapes or combine several shapes together to make a more complex figure. You can modify many aspects of a shape including its fill color, line color, and line style, as well as add other effects like shadow and 3-D effects. Instead of changing individual attributes, you can apply a Quick Style to a shape. A **Quick Style** is a set of formatting options, including line style, fill color, and effects. You decide to draw some shapes on Slide 3 of your presentation that identify the different train routes offered by British Columbia Railways.

STEPS

1. **Click the Slide 3 thumbnail in the Slides tab**
   Slide 3 appears in the Slide pane.

2. **Press and hold [Shift], click the text object, then release [Shift]**
   The text object is selected. If you click a text object without pressing [Shift], a dotted selection box appears, indicating that the object is active and ready to accept text, but the text object itself is not selected.

3. **Position the pointer over the bottom-middle sizing handle, notice the pointer change to ↕, then drag the sizing handle up until the text object looks like Figure B-7**
   The text object decreases in size. When you position the pointer over a sizing handle, it changes to ↕. The pointer points in different directions depending on which sizing handle it is positioned over. When you drag a sizing handle, the pointer changes to ✛, and a faint gray outline appears, representing the size of the text object.

4. **Click the Shapes button in the Drawing group or click the More button ⊡ in the Drawing group**
   A gallery of shapes organized by type opens. Notice that there is a section at the top of the gallery where all of the recently used shapes are placed. ScreenTips help you identify the shapes.

5. **Click the Snip Diagonal Corner Rectangle shape ⬜ in the Rectangles section, position ✛ in the blank area of the slide below the text object, drag down and to the right to create the shape, as shown in Figure B-8, then release the mouse button**
   A rectangle shape appears on the slide, filled with the default color. To change the style of the shape, apply a Quick Style from the Shape Styles group.

6. **Click the Drawing Tools Format tab, click the More button ⊡ in the Shape Styles group, move the pointer over the styles in the gallery to review the effects on the shape, then click Subtle Effect — Olive Green, Accent 4**
   A light green Quick Style with coordinated gradient fill, line, and shadow color is applied to the shape.

7. **Click the Shape Outline button in the Shape Styles group, point to Weight, then move the pointer over the line weight options to review the effect on the shape**
   The outline line weight changes every time you move the pointer over a different effect.

8. **Click 2 ¼ pt, click in a blank area of the slide, then save your work**

FIGURE B-7: Resized text object

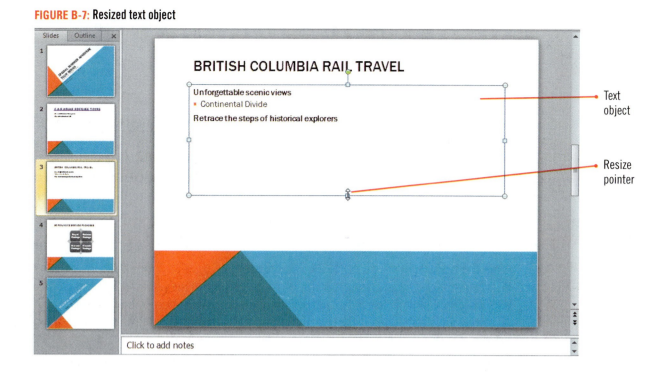

Text object

Resize pointer

FIGURE B-8: Slide showing Snip Diagonal Corner Rectangle shape

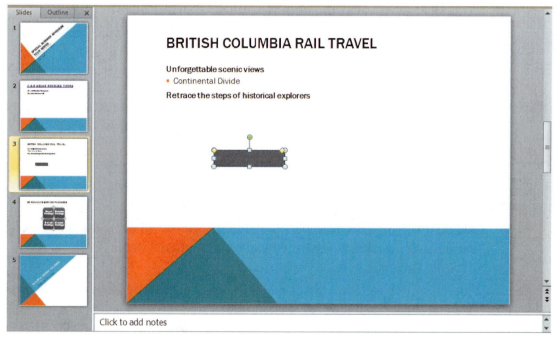

Changing the size and position of shapes

Usually when you resize a shape you can simply drag one of the sizing handles around the outside of the shape, but sometimes you may need to resize a shape more precisely. When you select a shape, the Drawing Tools Format tab appears on the Ribbon, offering you many different formatting options including some sizing commands located in the Size group. The Width and Height commands in the Size group allow you to change the width and height of a shape. You also have the option to open the Size and Position dialog box, which allows you to change the size of a shape, as well as the rotation, scale, and position of a shape on the slide.

Editing and Duplicating Shapes

Once you have created a shape you still have the ability to refine the aspects of the object. PowerPoint allows you to adjust various aspects of shapes to help change the look of them. For example, if you create a shape with an arrowhead but the head of the arrow does not look quite like you want it to look, you can change it. You can also add text to most PowerPoint shapes, and you can move or copy shapes. You want three identical rectangles on Slide 3. You first change the shape of the rectangle you've already created, and then you make copies of it.

STEPS

1. **Click the rectangle shape on Slide 3 to select it**

   In addition to sizing handles, two other types of handles appear on the selected object. You use the **adjustment handle**—a small yellow diamond—to change the appearance of an object. The adjustment handle appears next to the most prominent feature of the object, like the diagonal sides of the rectangle in this case. You use the **rotate handle**—a small green circle—to manually rotate the object.

2. **Drag the left-middle sizing handle on the rectangle shape to the right approximately 1/4", then release the mouse button**

QUICK TIP

You can easily display or hide gridlines by clicking the Gridlines check box in the Show group on the View tab.

3. **Position the pointer over the middle of the selected rectangle shape so that it changes to ⊹, then drag the rectangle shape so that the rectangle aligns with the left edge of the text in the text object as shown in Figure B-9**

   A semitransparent copy of the shape appears as you move the rectangle shape to help you position it. PowerPoint uses gridlines to align objects; it forces objects to "snap" to the grid. To turn the snap-to-grid feature off while dragging objects, press and hold [Alt]. Make any needed adjustments to the rectangle shape position so it looks similar to Figure B-9.

TROUBLE

To make precise adjustments, press and hold [Alt], then drag the adjustment handle.

4. **Position the pointer over the right adjustment handle on the rectangle shape so that it changes to ▷, then drag the adjustment handle all the way to the left**

   The rectangle shape appearance changes.

5. **Position ⊹ over the rectangle shape, then press and hold [Ctrl]**

   The pointer changes to ⊹₊, indicating that PowerPoint makes a copy of the rectangle shape when you drag the mouse.

6. **Holding [Ctrl], drag the rectangle shape to the right until the rectangle shape copy is in a blank area of the slide, release the mouse button, then release [Ctrl]**

   An identical copy of the rectangle shape appears on the slide.

QUICK TIP

All shape objects use the dotted alignment line to help you align shapes to an object's top, bottom, or side.

7. **With the second rectangle shape still selected, repeat Steps 5 and 6 to create a third rectangle shape, then type Northern Route**

   A dotted line appears through the center of the shapes identifying the centerline of the shapes and helps you align the shapes. The text appears in the selected rectangle shape. The text is now part of the shape, so if you move or rotate the shape, the text moves with it. Compare your screen with Figure B-10.

8. **Click the middle rectangle shape, type Western Pass, click the left rectangle shape, type Explorer's Trail, then click in a blank area of the slide**

   Clicking a blank area of the slide deselects all objects that are selected.

9. **Save your work**

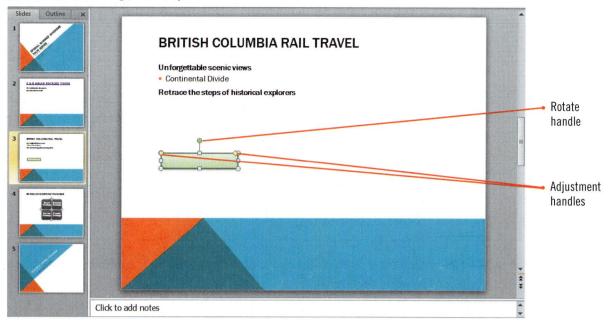

FIGURE B-10: Slide showing duplicated shapes

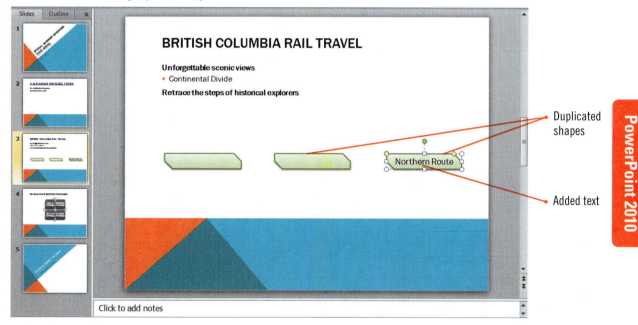

Understanding PowerPoint objects

Every object on a slide, whether it is a text object, a shape, a chart, a picture, or any other object, is stacked on the slide in the order it was created. So, for example, if you add three shapes to a slide, the first shape you create is on the bottom of the stack, and the last shape you create is on the top of the stack. Each object on a slide can be moved up or down in the stack depending on how you want the objects to look on the slide. To move an object to the front of the stack, select the object, then click the Bring Forward button in the Arrange group on the Drawing Tools Format tab. To move an object to the back of the stack, click the Send Backward button in the Arrange group on the Drawing Tools Format tab. You can also open the Selection and Visibility pane by clicking the Selection Pane button in the Arrange group to view and rearrange all of the objects on the slide.

Aligning and Grouping Objects

After you are finished creating and modifying your objects, you can position them accurately on the slide to achieve the look you want. Using the Align commands in the Arrange group, you can align objects relative to each other by snapping them to a grid of evenly spaced vertical and horizontal lines. The Group command **groups** objects into one object, which secures their relative position to each other and makes it easy to edit and move them. The Distribute commands found with the Align commands evenly space objects horizontally or vertically relative to each other or the slide. You are ready to position and group the arrow shapes on Slide 3 to make the slide look consistent and planned.

STEPS

QUICK TIP

To add a new guide to the slide, press [Ctrl], then drag an existing guide. The original guide remains in place as you move the new guide. Drag a guide off the slide to delete it.

1. **Right-click a blank area of the slide, then click Grid and Guides on the shortcut menu**

   The Grid and Guides dialog box opens.

2. **Click the Display drawing guides on screen check box, then click OK**

   The PowerPoint guides appear as dotted lines on the slide and intersect at the center of the slide. They help you position a rectangle shape.

3. **Position ▷ over the horizontal guide in a blank area of the slide, press and hold the mouse button until the pointer changes to a measurement guide, then drag the guide down until the guide position box reads 1.25**

4. **Position ⬆ over the Explorer's Trail rectangle shape (not over the text in the shape), then drag the shape so that the bottom edge of the shape touches the horizontal guide as shown in Figure B-11**

   The rectangle shape attaches or "snaps" to the horizontal guide.

5. **With the Explorer's Trail shape selected, press and hold [Shift], click the other two rectangle shapes, then release [Shift]**

   All three shapes are now selected.

6. **Click the Drawing Tools Format tab on the Ribbon, click the Align button in the Arrange group, then click Align Bottom**

   The shapes are now aligned horizontally along their bottom edges. The higher shapes move down and align with the bottom shape.

7. **Click the Align button, then click Distribute Horizontally**

   The shapes are now distributed equally between themselves.

QUICK TIP

Rulers can help you align objects. To display the rulers, position the pointer in a blank area of the slide, right-click, then click Ruler on the shortcut menu.

8. **Click the Group button in the Arrange group, click Group, then press [Left Arrow] or [Right Arrow] until the Rotate handle is on or very near the vertical grid line as shown in Figure B-12**

   The objects group to form one object without losing their individual attributes. Notice that the sizing handles and rotate handle now appear on the outer edge of the grouped object, not around each individual object.

9. **Drag the horizontal guide up until the guide position box reads 0.00, click the View tab on the Ribbon, then click the Guides check box in the Show group**

   The guides are no longer displayed on the slide

10. **Click a blank area of the slide, then save your work**

FIGURE B-11: Repositioned shape

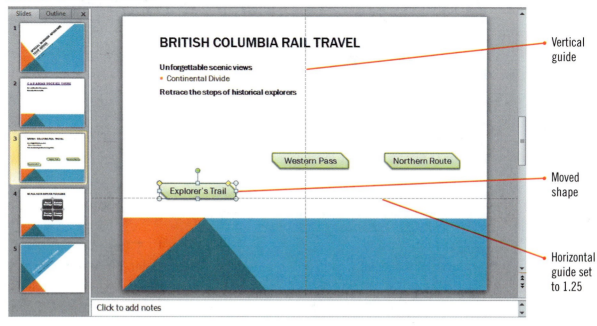

Vertical guide

Moved shape

Horizontal guide set to 1.25

FIGURE B-12: Aligned and grouped shapes

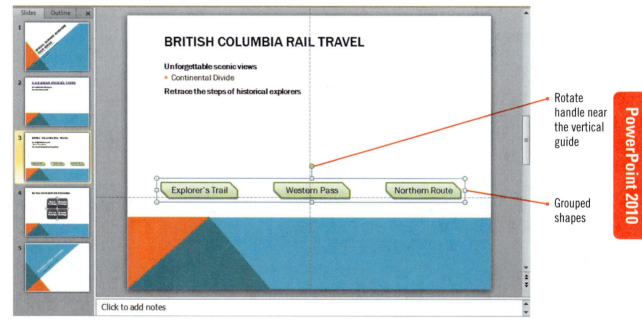

Rotate handle near the vertical guide

Grouped shapes

Distributing objects

There are two ways to **distribute** objects in PowerPoint: relative to each other and relative to the slide edge. If you choose to distribute objects relative to each other, PowerPoint evenly divides the empty space between all of the selected objects. When distributing objects in relation to the slide, PowerPoint evenly splits the empty space from slide edge to slide edge between the selected objects. To distribute objects relative to each other, click the Align button in the Arrange group on the Drawing Tools Format tab, then click Align Selected Objects. To distribute objects relative to the slide, click the Align button in the Arrange group on the Drawing Tools Format tab, then click Align to Slide.

Adding Slide Headers and Footers

Header and footer text, such as a company, school or product name, the slide number, and the date, can give your slides a polished look and make it easier for your audience to follow your presentation. On slides, you can add text to the footer; however, notes or handouts can include both header and footer text. Footer information that you apply to the slides of your presentation is visible in the PowerPoint views and when you print the slides. Notes and handouts header and footer text is visible when you print notes pages, handouts, and the outline. You add footer text to the slides of the Canadian train tour presentation to make it easier for the audience to follow.

STEPS

1. **Click the Insert tab on the Ribbon, then click the Header & Footer button in the Text group**

   The Header and Footer dialog box opens, as shown in Figure B-13. The Header and Footer dialog box has two tabs: a Slide tab and a Notes and Handouts tab. The Slide tab is selected. There are three types of footer text, Date and time, Slide number, and Footer. The rectangles at the bottom of the Preview box identify the default position and status of the three types of footer text placeholders on the slides.

2. **Click the Date and time check box to select it**

   The date and time suboptions are now available to select. The Update automatically date and time option button is selected by default. This option updates the date and time every time you open or print the file.

3. **Click the Update automatically list arrow, then click the eighth option in the list**

   The time is added to the date.

4. **Click the Slide number check box, click the Footer check box, then type your name**

   The Preview box now shows that all three footer placeholders are selected.

5. **Click the Don't show on title slide check box**

   Selecting this check box prevents the footer information you entered in the Header and Footer dialog box from appearing on the title slide.

6. **Click Apply to All**

   The dialog box closes and the footer information is applied to all of the slides in your presentation except the title slide. Compare your screen to Figure B-14.

7. **Click the Slide 1 thumbnail in the Slides tab, then click the Header & Footer button in the Text group**

   The Header and Footer dialog box opens again.

8. **Click the Don't show on title slide check box to deselect it, click the Footer check box, then select the text in the Footer text box**

9. **Type World's foremost traveling experience, click Apply, then save your work**

   Only the text in the Footer text box appears on the title slide. Clicking Apply applies the footer information to just the current slide.

FIGURE B-13: Header and Footer dialog box

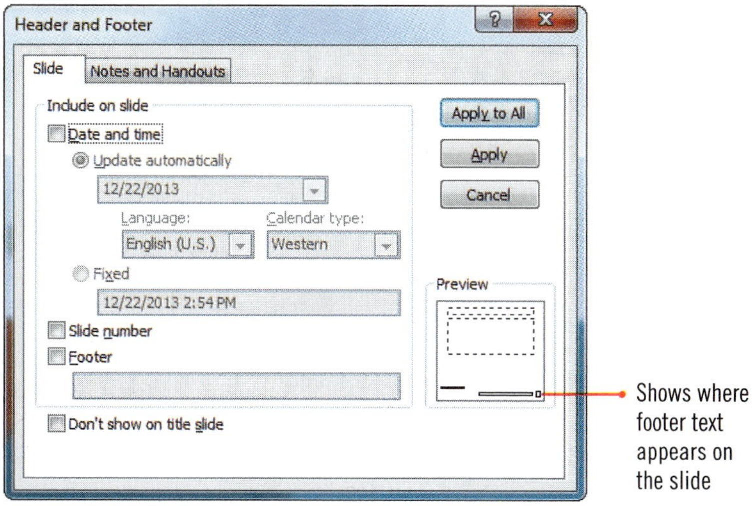

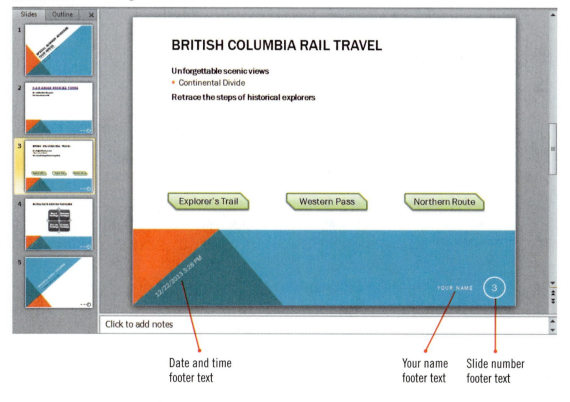

Shows where footer text appears on the slide

FIGURE B-14: Slide showing footer information

Date and time footer text

Your name footer text

Slide number footer text

Entering and printing notes

You can add notes to your slides when there are certain facts you want to remember during a presentation or when there is information you want to hand out to your audience. Notes do not appear on the slides when you run a slide show. Use the Notes pane in Normal view or Notes Page view to enter notes for your slides. To enter text notes on a slide, click in the Notes pane, then type. If you want to insert graphics as notes, you must use Notes Page view. To open Notes Page view, click the View tab on the Ribbon, then click the Notes Page button in the Presentation Views group. You can print your notes by clicking the File tab to open Backstage view then clicking Print. Click the Full Page Slides list arrow in the Settings section (this button retains the last setting for what was printed previously so it might differ) to open the gallery, and then click Notes Pages. Once you verify your print settings, click the Print button. Notes pages can be a good handout to give your audience to use during the presentation. If you don't enter any notes in the Notes pane, and print the notes pages, the slides print as thumbnails with blank lines to the right of the thumbnails to hand write notes.

PowerPoint 2010

Using Proofing and Language Tools

As your work on the presentation file nears completion, you need to review and proofread your slides thoroughly for errors. You can use the spell-checking feature in PowerPoint to check for and correct spelling errors. This feature compares the spelling of all the words in your presentation against the words contained in PowerPoint's electronic dictionary. You still must proofread your presentation for punctuation, grammar, and word-usage errors because the spell checker recognizes only misspelled and unknown words, not misused words. For example, the spell checker would not identify the word "last" as an error, even if you had intended to type the word "cast." PowerPoint also includes language tools that translate words or phrases from your default language into another language using the Microsoft Translator. You're finished working on the presentation for now, so it's a good time to check spelling. You then experiment with language translation because the final presentation will be translated into French.

STEPS

TROUBLE

If your spell checker finds another word, such as your name on Slide 1, click Ignore All in the spelling dialog box.

1. **Click the Review tab on the Ribbon, then click the Spelling button in the Proofing group**

   PowerPoint begins to check the spelling in your presentation. When PowerPoint finds a misspelled word or a word it doesn't recognize, the Spelling dialog box opens, as shown in Figure B-15. In this case, PowerPoint identifies the misspelled word on Slide 4 and suggests you replace it with the correctly spelled word "Exclusive."

2. **Click Change**

   PowerPoint changes the misspelled word and then continues to check the rest of the presentation for errors. If PowerPoint finds any other words it does not recognize, either change or ignore them. When the spell checker finishes checking your presentation, the Spelling dialog box closes, and an alert box opens with a message that the spelling check is complete.

QUICK TIP

The spell checker does not check the text in inserted pictures or objects.

3. **Click OK, click the Slide 1 thumbnail in the Slides tab, then save your presentation**

   The alert box closes. Now you need to see how the language translation feature works.

4. **Click the Translate button in the Language group, then click Choose Translation Language**

   The Translation Language Options dialog box opens.

5. **Click the Translate to list arrow, click French (France), then click OK**

   The Translation Language Options dialog box closes.

6. **Click the Translate button in the Language group, click Mini Translator [French(France)], click anywhere in the footer text object, then select all of the text**

   The Microsoft Translator begins to analyze the selected text and a semitransparent Microsoft Translator box appears below the text.

QUICK TIP

To copy the translated text to a slide, click the Copy button at the bottom of the Microsoft Translator box, right-click the slide, then click a Paste option.

7. **Move the pointer over the Microsoft Translator box**

   A French translation of the text appears as shown in Figure B-16. The translation language setting remains in effect until you reset it.

8. **Click the Translate button in the Language group, click Choose Translation Language, click the Translate to list arrow, click Arabic, click OK, click the Translate button again, then click Mini Translator [Arabic]**

   The Mini Translator is turned off and the translation language is restored to the default setting.

9. **Submit your presentation to your instructor, then exit PowerPoint**

FIGURE B-15: Spelling dialog box

FIGURE B-15: Spelling dialog box

Selected word from Suggestions list — Unrecognized word

Suggestions list

FIGURE B-16: Slide showing translated text

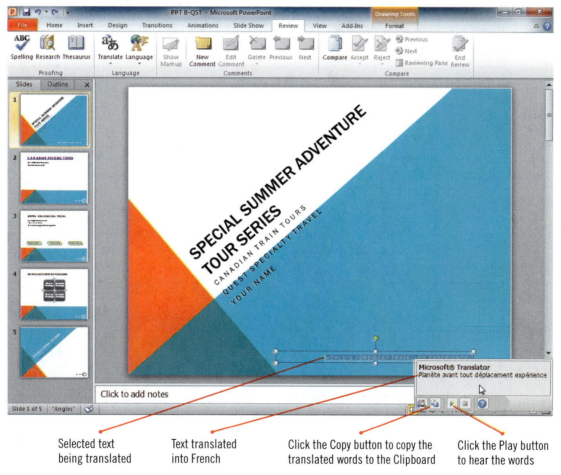

Selected text being translated — Text translated into French — Click the Copy button to copy the translated words to the Clipboard — Click the Play button to hear the words

PowerPoint 2010

Checking spelling as you type

PowerPoint checks your spelling as you type. If you type a word that is not in the electronic dictionary, a wavy red line appears under it. To correct an error, right-click the misspelled word, then review the suggestions, which appear in the shortcut menu. You can select a suggestion, add the word you typed to your custom dictionary, or ignore it. To turn off automatic spell checking, click the File tab, then click Options to open the PowerPoint Options dialog box. Click the Proofing button, then click the Check spelling as you type check box

to deselect it. To temporarily hide the wavy red lines, click the Hide spelling errors check box to select it. Contextual spelling in PowerPoint identifies common grammatically misused words, for example, if you type the word "their" and the correct word is "there," PowerPoint will identify the mistake and place a wavy blue line under the word. To turn contextual spelling on or off, click the Proofing button in the PowerPoint Options dialog box, then click the Use contextual spelling check box.

Practice

For current SAM information, including versions and content details, visit SAM Central (http://www.cengage.com/samcentral). If you have a SAM user profile, you may have access to hands-on instruction, practice, and assessment of the skills covered in this unit. Since various versions of SAM are supported throughout the life of this text, check with your instructor for the correct instructions and URL/Web site for accessing assignments.

Concepts Review

Label each element of the PowerPoint window shown in Figure B-17.

FIGURE B-17

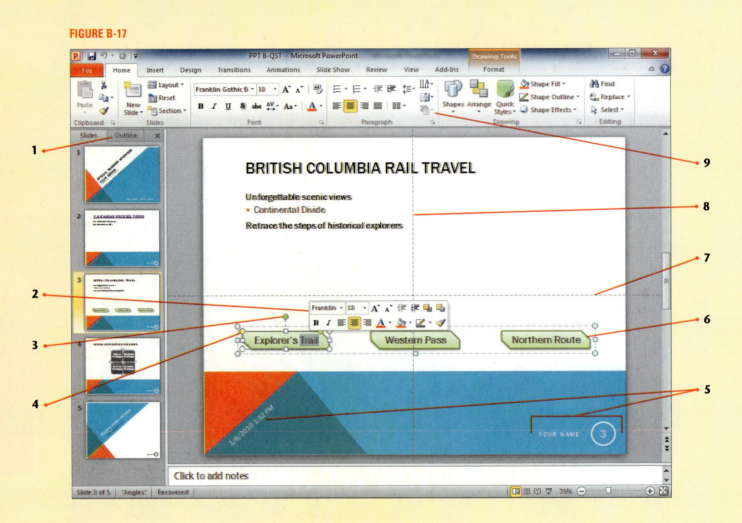

Match each term with the statement that best describes it.

10. **Quick Style**
11. **Rotate handle**
12. **Distribute**
13. **Mini toolbar**
14. **SmartArt graphic**
15. **Group**

a. Use to space objects evenly
b. A diagram that visually illustrates text
c. Use to manually turn an object
d. Combines multiple objects into one object
e. Use to format selected text
f. A preset combination of formatting options that you apply to an object

Select the best answer from the list of choices.

16. **Which of the following statements is *not* true about the Outline tab?**
    a. Each line of indented text creates a new slide title.
    b. You can enter text directly.
    c. It is organized using headings and subpoints.
    d. Headings are the same as slide titles.

17. **What appears just above text when it is selected?**
    a. QuickStyles
    b. Option button
    c. Mini toolbar
    d. AutoFit Options button

18. **What does the adjustment handle do to a shape?**
    a. Changes the appearance of a shape
    b. Changes the style of a shape
    c. Changes the size of a shape
    d. Changes the shape to another design

19. **A professional-quality diagram that visually illustrates text best describes which of the following?**
    a. A shape
    b. A SmartArt graphic
    c. A slide layout
    d. A QuickStyle object

20. **Which of the following is not *true* about checking spelling in PowerPoint?**
    a. The spell checker identifies unknown words as misspelled.
    b. Spelling is checked as you type.
    c. You can fix a misspelled word by right-clicking it and selecting a correct word.
    d. All misused words are automatically corrected.

21. **What is *not* true about grouped objects?**
    a. Grouped objects have one rotate handle.
    b. Sizing handles appear around the grouped object.
    c. Each object has individual sizing handles and a rotate handle.
    d. Grouped objects act as one object.

22. **What do objects snap to when you move them?**
    a. Slide edges
    b. Hidden grid
    c. Drawing lines
    d. Anchor points

Skills Review

1. **Enter text in the Outline tab.**
   a. Open the presentation PPT B-2.pptx from the drive and folder where you store your Data Files, then save it as **PPT B-PoolClean Pro**. The completed presentation is shown in Figure B-18.
   b. Create a new slide after Slide 2 with the Title and Content layout.
   c. Open the Outline tab, then type **Major Marketing Avenues**.
   d. Press [Enter], press [Tab], type **Online Forums**, press [Enter], type **Instant Messengers**, press [Enter], then type **Online Classifieds**.
   e. Move Slide 3 above Slide 2.
   f. Switch back to the Slides tab.
   g. Save your changes.

2. **Format text.**
   a. Go to Slide 1.
   b. Select the name **D.T. Wittenger**, then move the pointer over the Mini toolbar.
   c. Click the Font Color list arrow, then click Dark Blue, Text 2 under Theme Colors.

FIGURE B-18

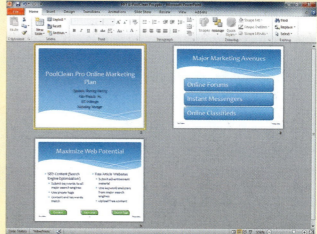

   d. Select the text object, then change all of the text to the color Dark Blue, Text 2.

   e. Click the Font Size list arrow, then click 24.

   f. Click the Italic button.

   g. Click the Character Spacing button, then click Tight.

   h. Save your changes.

3. Convert text to SmartArt.

   a. Click the text object on Slide 2.

   b. Click the Convert to SmartArt Graphic button, then apply the Vertical Block List graphic layout to the text object.

   c. Click the More button in the Layouts group, click More Layouts, click List in the Choose a SmartArt Graphic dialog box, then click Vertical Bullet List.

   d. Click the More button in the SmartArt Styles group, then apply the Intense Effect style to the graphic.

   e. Close the text pane if necessary, then click outside the SmartArt graphic in an empty part of the slide.

   f. Save your changes.

4. Insert and modify shapes.

   a. Go to Slide 3.

   b. Press [Shift], click both text objects, release [Shift], then drag the bottom-middle sizing handle up to decrease the size of the text objects.

   c. Click the Shapes button in the Drawing group, then insert the Round Diagonal Corner Rectangle shape from the Shapes gallery similar to the one in Figure B-19.

   d. On the Drawing Tools Format tab, click the More button in the Shape Styles group, then click Light 1 Outline, Colored Fill – Green, Accent 3.

   e. Click the Shape Effects button in the Shape Styles group, point to Shadow, then click Offset Diagonal Bottom Right.

   f. Click the Shape Outline button in the Shape Styles group, then click Black, Text 1, Lighter 25%.

   g. Click a blank area of the slide, then save your changes.

5. Edit and duplicate shapes.

   a. Select the rectangle shape, then drag the left adjustment handle all the way to the right.

   b. Drag the rectangle shape so it lines up with the text in the left text object about ½ inch from the bottom of the slide.

   c. Click the Rotate button in the Arrange group, then click Flip Horizontal.

   d. Using [Ctrl] make two copies of the rectangle shape.

   e. Type **Search Tags** in the right rectangle shape, type **Keywords** in the middle rectangle shape, then type **Content** in the left rectangle shape.

   f. Click a blank area of the slide, then save your changes.

6. Align and group objects.

   a. Select the right rectangle shape, press [Shift], then move it to so it lines up with the right edge of the text in the right text object.

   b. Select all three rectangle shapes.

   c. Click the Drawing Tools Format tab if necessary, click the Align button, then click Align Bottom.

   d. Click the Align button in the Arrange group, then click Distribute Horizontally.

   e. Group all three rectangles together, then display the drawing guides on the screen.

FIGURE B-19

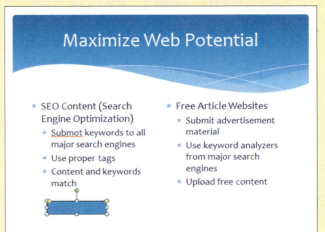

Skills Review (continued)

f. Move the horizontal guide down until 3.17 appears, then press [Up Arrow] or press [Down Arrow] until the bottom of the rectangle shapes are on or near the horizontal guide. Compare your screen to Figure B-20.

g. Remove the drawing guides from your screen, then save your work.

7. Add slide headers and footers.

FIGURE B-20

a. Open the Header and Footer dialog box.

b. On the Slide tab, click the Date and time check box to select it, click the Fixed option button, then type today's date in the Fixed text box.

c. Add the slide number to the footer.

d. Type your name in the Footer text box.

e. Apply the footer to all of the slides except the title slide.

f. Open the Header and Footer dialog box again, then click the Notes and Handouts tab.

g. Type today's date in the Fixed text box.

h. Type the name of your class in the Header text box, then click the Page number check box.

i. Type your name in the Footer text box.

j. Apply the header and footer information to all the notes and handouts.

k. Save your changes.

8. Use proofing and language tools.

a. Check the spelling of the document, and change any misspelled words. Ignore any words that are correctly spelled but that the spell checker doesn't recognize. There is at least one misspelled word in the presentation.

b. Move to Slide 3, then set the Mini Translator language to Russian.

c. View the Russian translation of two or three individual words and a phrase on Slide 3.

d. Choose one other language (or as many as you want), translate words or phrases on the slide, reset the default language to Arabic, then turn off the Mini Translator.

e. Save your changes, submit your presentation to your instructor, close the presentation, then exit PowerPoint.

Independent Challenge 1

You are the Director of the Performing Arts Center in Council Bluffs, Iowa, and one of your many duties is to raise funds to cover operation costs. One of the primary ways you do this is by speaking to businesses, community clubs, and other organizations throughout the Council Bluffs region. Every year you speak to many organizations, where you give a short presentation detailing what the theater center plans to do for the coming season. You need to continue working on the presentation you started already.

If you have a SAM 2010 user profile, an autogradable SAM version of this assignment may be available at http://www.cengage.com/sam2010. Check with your instructor to confirm that this assignment is available in SAM. To use the SAM version of this assignment, log into the SAM 2010 Web site and download the instruction and start files.

a. Start PowerPoint, open the presentation PPT B-3.pptx from the drive and folder where you store your Data Files, and save it as **PPT B-Arts Center**.

b. Use the Outline tab to enter the following as bulleted text on the Commitment to Excellence slide:

Study

Diligence

Testing

Excellence

c. Apply the Technic design theme to the presentation.

d. Change the font color of each play name on Slide 3 to Gold, Accent 2, Lighter 40%.

e. Change the bulleted text on Slide 5 to the Vertical Accent List SmartArt graphic layout, then apply the Moderate Effect SmartArt Style.

Independent Challenge 1 (continued)

Advanced Challenge Exercise

- Open the Notes Page view.
- To at least two slides, add notes that relate to the slide content that you think would be important when giving this presentation.
- Save the presentation as **Arts Center ACE** to the drive and folder where you store your Data Files. When submitting the presentation to your instructor, submit the Notes Pages.

f. Check the spelling in the presentation (there is at least one spelling error), then view the presentation in Slide Show view.

g. Add your name as a footer on the notes and handouts, then save your changes.

h. Submit your presentation to your instructor, close your presentation, then exit PowerPoint.

Independent Challenge 2

You are a manager for Jess Hauser Investments Inc., a financial services company. You have been asked by your boss to develop a presentation outlining important details and aspects of the mortgage process to be used at a financial seminar.

a. Start PowerPoint, open the presentation PPT B-4.pptx from the drive and folder where you store your Data Files, and save it as **PPT B-Hauser**.

b. Apply the Hardcover design theme to the presentation.

c. On Slide 4 select the three shapes, Banks, Mortgage Bankers, and Private Investors, then using the Align command distribute them vertically and align them to their left edges.

d. On Slide 4 select the three shapes, Borrower, Mortgage Broker, and Mortgage Bankers, then using the Align command distribute them horizontally and align them to their bottom edges.

e. Select all of the shapes, then apply Intense Effect – Black, Dark 1 from the Shape Styles group, then move the shapes down as shown in Figure B-21.

FIGURE B-21

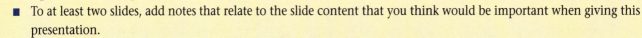

f. Using the Arrow shape from the Shapes gallery, draw a 2 ¼-pt arrow between all of the shapes. (*Hint*: Draw one arrow shape, change the line weight to 2 ¼-pt using the Shape Outline button, then duplicate the shape.)

g. Create a sixth slide to end the presentation, then type the following information in the Outline tab:

Program Summary
    We will find the right loan for you
    You will be able to afford your loan
    You will save money with our loan
    No government interference

h. Check the spelling in the presentation, view the presentation in Slide Show view, then view the slides in Slide Sorter view.

i. Add the page number and your name as a footer on the notes and handouts, then save your changes.

j. Submit your presentation to your instructor, close your presentation, then exit PowerPoint.

Independent Challenge 3

You are an independent distributor of natural foods in Spokane, Washington. Your business, Pacific Coast Natural Foods, has grown progressively since its inception 10 years ago, but sales have leveled off over the last 12 months. In an effort to stimulate growth, you decide to purchase Idaho Foods Inc., a natural food dealer in Idaho, which would allow your company to begin expanding into surrounding states. Use PowerPoint to develop a presentation that you can use to gain a financial backer for the acquisition. Create your own information for the presentation.

a. Start PowerPoint, create a new presentation, then apply the Thatch design theme to the presentation.
b. Type **A Plan for Growth** as the main title on the title slide, and **Pacific Coast Natural Foods** as the subtitle.
c. Save the presentation as **PPT B-Pacific Coast** to the drive and folder where you store your Data Files.
d. Add five more slides with the following titles: Slide 2-**Background**; Slide 3-**Current Situation**; Slide 4-**Acquisition Goals**; Slide 5-**Funding Required**; Slide 6-**Our Management Team**.
e. Enter appropriate text into the text placeholders of the slides. Use both the Slide pane and the Outline tab to enter text.
f. Convert text on one slide to a SmartArt graphic, then apply the SmartArt graphic style Inset Effect.

Advanced Challenge Exercise

- Click the Replace list arrow in the Editing group on the Home tab, then click Replace Fonts.
- Replace the Tw Cen MT font with the Eras Medium ITC font.
- Save the presentation as **PPT B-Pacific Coast ACE** to the drive and folder where you store your Data Files.

g. Check the spelling in the presentation, view the presentation as a slide show, then view the slides in Slide Sorter view.
h. Add the slide number and your name as a footer on the slides, then save your changes.
i. Submit your presentation to your instructor, close your presentation, then exit PowerPoint.

Real Life Independent Challenge

Your computer instructor at City Junior College has been asked by the department head to convert his Computer Basics 101 course into an accelerated course that both students and professional working people can take. Your instructor has asked you to help him create a presentation for the class that he can post on the Internet and use as a promotional tool at local businesses. Most of the raw information is already on the slides, you primarily need to jazz it up by adding a theme and some text formatting.

a. Start PowerPoint, open the presentation PPT B-5.pptx from drive and folder where you store your data files, and save it as **PPT B-Course 101**.
b. Add a new slide after the Course Facts slide with the same layout, type **Course Details** in the title text placeholder, then enter the following as bulleted text in the Outline tab:
   Unix/Information Systems
   Networking
   Applied Methods
   Technology Solutions
   Software Design
   Applications
c. Apply the Paper design theme to the presentation.
d. Select the title text object on Slide 1 (*Hint*: Press [Shift] to select the whole object), then change the text color to Yellow.
e. Change the font of the title text object to Century Gothic.
f. Click the subtitle text object, click the AutoFit Options button, then click Stop Fitting Text to This Placeholder.
g. Change the text on Slide 4 to a SmartArt graphic. Use an appropriate diagram type for a list.
h. Change the style of the SmartArt diagram using one of the SmartArt Styles, then view the presentation in Slide Show view.
i. Add the slide number and your name as a footer on the notes and handouts, then save your changes.
j. Submit your presentation to your instructor, close your presentation, then exit PowerPoint.

Visual Workshop

Create the presentation shown in Figures B-22 and B-23. Add today's date as the date on the title slide. Save the presentation as **PPT B-Ag Trade** to the drive and folder where you store your Data Files. (*Hint*: The SmartArt style used for the SmartArt is a 3-D style.) Review your slides in Slide Show view, then add your name as a footer to the notes and handouts. Submit your presentation to your instructor, save your changes, close the presentation, then exit PowerPoint.

FIGURE B-22

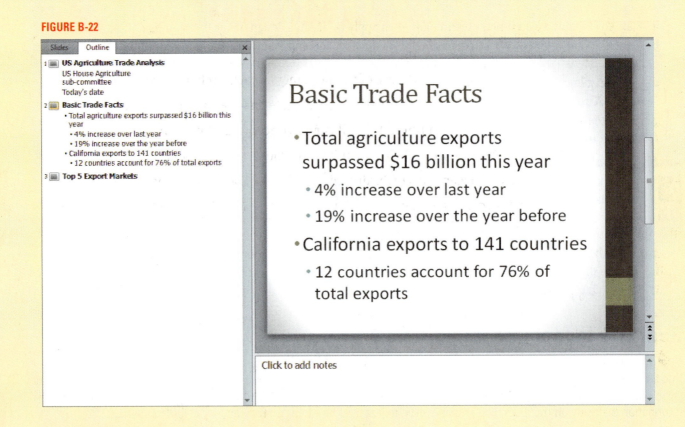

FIGURE B-23

Inserting Objects into a Presentation

A good presenter will make use of visual elements, such as charts, graphics, and photographs, in conjunction with text to help communicate the presentation message. Visual elements keep the presentation interesting, illustrate concepts, and help the audience focus on what the presenter is saying.  In this unit, you continue working on the presentation by inserting visual elements, including clip art, a photograph, and a chart, into the presentation. You format these objects using PowerPoint's powerful object-editing features.

OBJECTIVES

Insert text from Microsoft Word

Insert clip art

Insert and style a picture

Insert a text box

Insert a chart

Enter and edit chart data

Insert a table

Insert and format WordArt

Inserting Text from Microsoft Word

It is easy to insert documents saved in Microsoft Word format (.docx), Rich Text Format (.rtf), plain text format (.txt), and HTML format (.htm) into a PowerPoint presentation. If you have an outline saved in a document file, you can import it into PowerPoint to create a new presentation or create additional slides in an existing presentation. When you import a document into a presentation, PowerPoint creates an outline structure based on the styles in the document. For example, a Heading 1 style in the Word document becomes a slide title and a Heading 2 style becomes the first level of text in a bulleted list. If you insert a plain text format document into a presentation, PowerPoint creates an outline based on the tabs at the beginning of the document's paragraphs. Paragraphs without tabs become slide titles and paragraphs with one tab indent become first-level text in bulleted lists. You have a Microsoft Word document with information about the different Canadian train routes that you want to insert into your presentation to create several new slides.

STEPS

1. **Start PowerPoint, open the presentation PPT C-1.pptx from the drive and folder where you store your Data Files, save it as PPT C-QST, click the Outline tab, then click the Slide 3 icon ▣ in the Outline tab**

   Slide 3 appears in the Slide pane. Clicking a slide icon in the Outline tab highlights the slide text indicating the slide is selected. Before you insert an outline into a presentation, you need to determine where you want the new slides to be placed. You want the text from the Word document inserted as new slides after Slide 3.

2. **Click the New Slide list arrow in the Slides group, then click Slides from Outline**

   The Insert Outline dialog box opens.

3. **Navigate to the drive and folder where you store your Data Files, click the Word document file PPT C-2.docx, then click Insert**

   Four new slides (4, 5, 6, and 7) are added to the presentation. See Figure C-1.

QUICK TIP
If your presentation has numerous slides, you can organize them into sections in the Slides tab. To create a section, click the slide in the Slides tab where you want the section to begin, click the Section button in the Slides group on the Home tab, then click Add Section.

4. **Read the text for the new Slide 4 in the Slide pane, then review the text on slides 5, 6, and 7 in the Outline tab**

   Information on Slide 7 refers to an obsolete train route and is not needed for this presentation.

5. **Click the Slides tab, then right-click the Slide 7 thumbnail in the Slides tab**

   A shortcut menu opens displaying related, or contextual, commands that are currently available.

6. **Click Delete Slide on the shortcut menu**

   Slide 7 is deleted, and the next slide down becomes the new Slide 7 and appears in the Slide pane.

7. **Click the Slide 6 thumbnail in the Slides tab, then drag it above Slide 5**

   Slide 6 and Slide 5 change places. You want the text of the inserted outline to adopt the presentation theme.

8. **Click the Slide 4 thumbnail, then click the Reset button in the Slides group**

   Notice that the font type and formatting attributes of the slide text changes to reflect the current theme fonts for the presentation. The Reset button resets the slide placeholders to their default position, size, and text formatting based on the Angles presentation design theme.

9. **Click the Slide 5 thumbnail, press and hold [Shift], click the Slide 6 thumbnail, release [Shift], click the Reset button, then click the Save button 🖫 on the Quick Access toolbar**

   Now all of the newly inserted slides have the same design theme as the rest of the presentation. Compare your screen to Figure C-2.

FIGURE C-1: Outline tab showing imported text

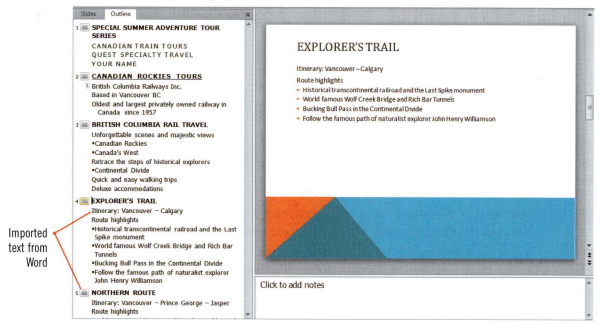

Imported text from Word

FIGURE C-2: Slide showing correct theme fonts

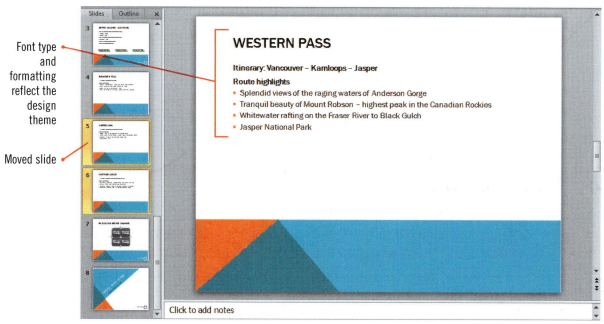

Font type and formatting reflect the design theme

Moved slide

Inserting slides from other presentations

To insert slides from another presentation into the current presentation, click the New Slide list arrow in the Slides group, then click Reuse Slides. The Reuse Slides task pane opens on the right side of the window. Click the Browse button, click Browse File in the drop down list, locate the presentation you want to use, then click Open. Click each slide you want to place in the current presentation. The new slides automatically take on the theme of the current presentation, unless you check the Keep source formatting check box. You can also copy slides from one presentation to another. Open both presentations, change the view of each presentation to Slide Sorter view or use the Arrange All command to see both presentations, select the desired slides, then copy and paste them (or use drag and drop) into the desired presentation.

Inserting Clip Art

In PowerPoint you have access to a collection of assorted types of media clips. The types of clips include illustrations, called **clip art**, photographs, animations, videos, and sounds. Clips are stored in the Microsoft **Clip Organizer**, a separate file index program, and are identified by descriptive keywords. The Clip Organizer is organized into folders called **collections** that you can customize by adding, moving, or deleting clips. Clip art and other media clips are available from many sources, including the Microsoft Office Web site and commercially available collections that you can purchase.  To enhance the QST presentation, you add a clip from the Clip Organizer to one of the slides, and then adjust its size and placement.

QUICK TIP

You can insert clip art anywhere on a slide by clicking the ClipArt button in the Images group on the Insert tab.

1. **Click the up scroll arrow in the Slides tab, click the Slide 2 thumbnail in the Slides tab, then click the Clip Art icon 🖼 in the Content placeholder**

   The Clip Art task pane opens. At the top of the task pane in the Search for text box, you enter a descriptive keyword to search for clips. If you want to limit or define the types of media clips PowerPoint searches for, click the Results should be list arrow, and then select or deselect specific media types.

2. **Verify that there is a check mark in the Include Office.com content check box, select any text in the Search for text box, type locomotive, then click the Results should be list arrow**

   You are only interested in finding clip art images that are located in the Illustrations category. Searching in only the categories you are interested in significantly reduces the number of media clips PowerPoint needs to search through to produce your results.

TROUBLE

If you don't see the clip shown in Figure C-3, select another one.

3. **Click the check boxes to remove all check marks, click the Illustrations check box, click the Go button, click the down scroll arrow, then click the clip art thumbnail shown in Figure C-3**

   The train clip appears in the content placeholder, and the Picture Tools Format tab is active on the Ribbon. Although you can change a clip's size by dragging a corner sizing handle, you can also **scale** it to change its size proportionally by a specific percentage or size.

4. **Select 2 in the Shape Width text box in the Size group, type 4, then press [Enter]**

   The train clip proportionally doubles in size. Notice the number in the Shape Height text box changes from 1.47 to 2.94.

5. **Click the Picture Border list arrow in the Picture Styles group, then click the Black, Text 1 color box in the top row**

   A black border appears around the train clip.

6. **Click the Picture Border list arrow, point to Weight, then click the 2 ¼ pt solid line style**

   The train clip now has a 2 ¼-point solid border, which creates a frame around the clip.

7. **Drag the train clip object to the middle of the blank area, click the Color button in the Adjust group, then click Orange, Accent color 2 Dark**

   You prefer the original placement and color of the train clip.

QUICK TIP

Click the Reset Picture button in the Adjust group to discard all the formatting changes.

8. **Click the Undo button list arrow 🔄 on the Quick Access toolbar, click Move Object, click a blank area of the slide, then save your changes**

   Notice that by using the Undo button list arrow, you can undo multiple actions in one step, in this case the Recolor Picture and the Move Object commands.

9. **Click the Results should be list arrow in the Clip Art task pane, click the All media types check box, click Go, then click the task pane Close button ❎**

   Now the next time you search for a clip, PowerPoint will search through all media types. Compare the slide on your screen to the slide shown in Figure C-4.

FIGURE C-3: Screen showing Clip Art task pane

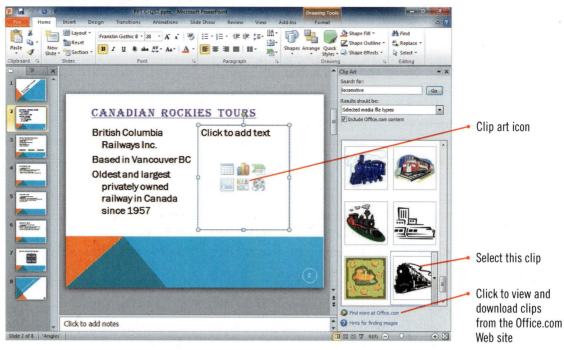

Clip art icon

Select this clip

Click to view and download clips from the Office.com Web site

FIGURE C-4: Slide with formatted train clip

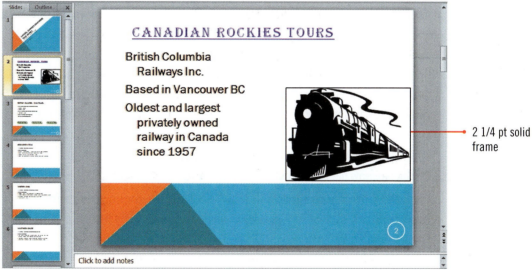

2 1/4 pt solid frame

Finding more clips online

If you can't find exactly what you want using the Clip Art task pane, you can easily find and download clips from the Office.com Web site. To get clips online, click the Find more at Office.com hyperlink at the bottom of the Clip Art task pane. If your computer is connected to the Internet, this will start your Web browser and automatically connect you to the Office.com Web site. You can search the site by keyword or browse by category type. Each clip you download is automatically inserted into the Clip Organizer and appears in the Clip Art task pane.

Inserting and Styling a Picture

In PowerPoint, a **picture** is defined as a digital photograph, a piece of line art or clip art, or other artwork that is created in another program. PowerPoint gives you the ability to insert 14 different types of pictures including JPEG File Interchange Format and BMP Windows Bitmap files into a PowerPoint presentation. As with all objects in PowerPoint, you can format and style inserted pictures to help them fit the theme of your presentation. You can also hide a portion of the picture you don't want to be seen by **cropping** it. The cropped portion of a picture remains a part of the picture file unless you delete the cropped portion by applying picture compression settings in the Compression Settings dialog box.  Using your digital camera, you took photographs during your train tours. In this lesson you insert a picture that you saved as a JPG file on your computer, and then you crop and style it to best fit the slide.

STEPS

QUICK TIP
You can also insert a picture by clicking the Picture button in the Images group on the Insert tab.

1. **Click the down scroll arrow in the Slides tab, click the Slide 8 thumbnail, then click the Insert Picture from File icon** 🖼 **in the content placeholder on the slide**
   The Insert Picture dialog box opens displaying the pictures available in the default Pictures library.

2. **Navigate to the drive and folder where you store your Data Files, select the picture file PPT C-3.jpg, then click Insert**
   The picture appears in the content placeholder on the slide, and the Picture Tools Format tab opens on the Ribbon. The picture would look better if you cropped some of the window reflection images off the right edge.

QUICK TIP
Click the Crop button list arrow to take advantage of other crop options including cropping to a shape from the Shapes gallery and cropping to a common photo size or aspect ratio.

3. **Click the Crop button in the Size group, then place the pointer over the lower-right corner cropping handle of the picture**
   The pointer changes to ⌐. When the Crop button is active, cropping handles appear next to the sizing handles.

4. **Drag the corner of the picture up and to the left as shown in Figure C-5, then press [Esc]**
   PowerPoint has a number of picture formatting options, and you decide to experiment with some of them.

5. **On the Picture Tools Format tab, click the More button** ⊡ **in the Picture Styles group, then click Compound Frame, Black (2nd row)**
   The picture now has a black frame.

6. **Click the Corrections button in the Adjust group, move your pointer over the thumbnails to see how the picture changes, then click Sharpen: 50% in the Sharpen and Soften section**
   The picture clarity is better.

7. **Click the Artistic Effects button in the Adjust group, move your pointer over the thumbnails to see how the picture changes, then click a blank area of the slide**
   The artistic effects are all interesting but none of them will work well for this picture. You decide to compress the picture to delete the cropped areas and make the file smaller.

QUICK TIP
If you want to apply an effect from the Artistic Effects gallery to a compressed picture, compress the picture first to maintain the best picture quality possible.

8. **Click the Compress Pictures button** 🖾 **in the Adjust group, make sure the Use document resolution option button is checked, then click OK**
   The cropped portions of the picture are deleted and the picture is compressed.

9. **Drag the lower-right sizing handle down so the right side of the picture increases in size and aligns with the right side of the slide number, click a blank area on the slide, then save your changes**
   Compare your screen to Figure C-6.

FIGURE C-5: Using the cropping pointer to crop a picture

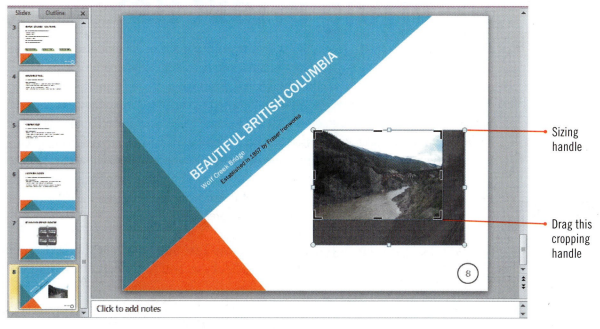

Sizing handle

Drag this cropping handle

FIGURE C-6: Cropped and styled picture

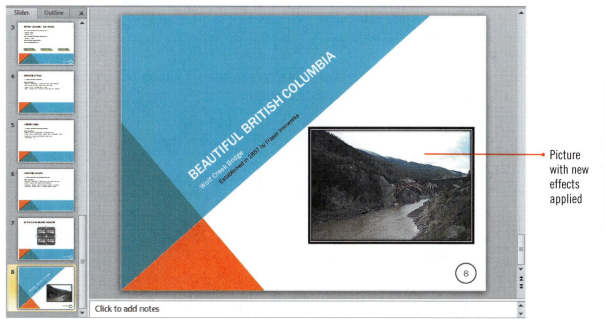

Picture with new effects applied

Things to know about picture compression

It's important to know that when you compress a picture you change the amount of detail in the picture, so it might look different than it did before the compression. Compressing a picture changes the amount of color used in the picture with no loss of quality. By default, all inserted pictures in PowerPoint are automatically compressed using the settings in the PowerPoint Options dialog box. To locate the compression settings, click the File tab, click Options, then click Advanced in the left pane. In the Image Size and Quality section, you can change picture compression settings or stop the automatic compression of pictures.

Inserting a Text Box

As you've already learned, you enter text on a slide using a title or content placeholder that is arranged on the slide based on a slide layout. Every so often you need additional text on a slide where the traditional placeholder does not place text effectively for your message. You can create an individual text box by clicking the Text Box button in the Text group on the Insert tab on the Ribbon. There are two types of text boxes that you can create: a text label, used for a small phrase where text doesn't automatically wrap to the next line inside the box; and a word-processing box, used for a sentence or paragraph where the text wraps inside the boundaries of the box. Either type of text box can be formatted and edited just like any other text object.  You decide to add a text box to the picture on Slide 8. You create a word-processing box on the slide, enter text, edit text, and then format the text.

STEPS

1. **Click the Insert tab on the Ribbon, click the Text Box button in the Text group, then move the pointer to the blank area of the slide above and to the left of the title text**
   The pointer changes to ↓.

2. **Drag down and toward the right about three inches to create a text box**
   When you begin dragging, an outline of the text box appears, indicating how large a text box you are drawing. After you release the mouse button, an insertion point appears inside the text box, in this case a word-processing box, indicating that you can enter text. The font and font style appear in the Font group on the Ribbon.

3. **Type On day 2 of the tour east of Kamloops 20 kilometers**
   Notice that the text box increases in size as your text wraps to a second line inside the text box. Your screen should look similar to Figure C-7. After entering the text you realize the sentence could be clearer if written differently.

4. **Drag ⌶ over the phrase 20 kilometers to select it, position ⌖ on top of the selected phrase, then press and hold the mouse button**
   The pointer changes to ⌖.

5. **Drag the selected words to the left of the word "east" in the text box, then release the mouse button**
   A light blue insertion line appears as you drag, indicating where PowerPoint places the text when you release the mouse button. The phrase "20 kilometers" moves before the word "east" and is still selected. Now fix the word spacing.

6. **Click between the words "kilometers" and "east" in the text, then press [Spacebar]**
   The words in the text box now have proper spacing.

7. **Move ⌶ to the edge of the text box, which changes to ⌖, click the text box border (changes to a solid line), then click the Italic button 𝐼 in the Font group**
   All of the text in the text box is italicized.

8. **Drag the right-middle sizing handle of the text box to the right until all the text fits on two lines, position ⌖ over the text box edge, then drag it above the picture**
   Your screen should look similar to Figure C-8.

9. **Click the Reading View button 📖 on the status bar, review the slide, press [Esc], then save your changes**

FIGURE C-7: New text object

New text
object ────────→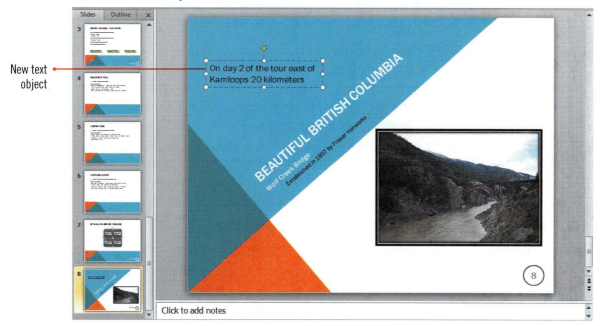

FIGURE C-8: Formatted text object

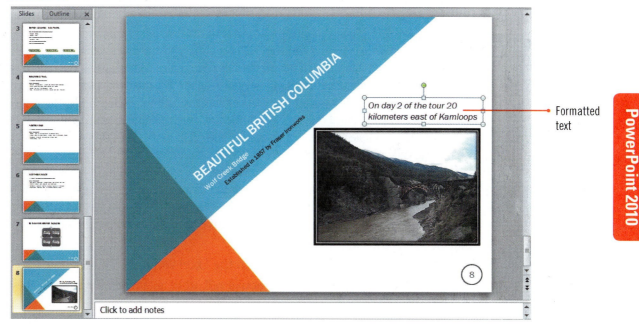

Formatted
text

Inserting a Chart

Frequently, the best way to communicate numerical information is with a visual aid such as a chart. If you have Microsoft Excel installed on your computer, PowerPoint uses Excel to create charts. If you don't have Excel installed, a charting program called **Microsoft Graph** opens that you can use to create charts for your slides. A **chart** is the graphical representation of numerical data. Every chart has a corresponding **worksheet** that contains the numerical data displayed by the chart. When you insert a chart object into PowerPoint, you are actually embedding it. An **embedded object** is one that is a part of your presentation (just like any other object you insert into PowerPoint) except that an embedded object's data source can be opened, in this case Excel, for editing purposes. Changes you make to an embedded object in PowerPoint using PowerPoint's features do not affect the data source for the data.  You insert a chart on a new slide.

STEPS

QUICK TIP
You can also add a chart to a slide by clicking the Insert Chart button in the Illustrations group on the Insert tab.

1. **Click Slide 7 in the Slides tab, then press [Enter]**
   Pressing [Enter] adds a new blank slide to your presentation with the slide layout of the selected slide, in this case the Title and Content slide layout.

2. **Click the Title placeholder, then type Vacation Comparison Survey**

3. **Click the Insert Chart icon 📊 in the Content placeholder**
   The Insert Chart dialog box opens as shown in Figure C-9. Each chart type includes a number of 2-D and 3-D styles. The Column chart type, for example, includes 19 different 2-D and 3-D styles. The 2-D Clustered Column chart is the default chart style. For a brief explanation of chart types, refer to Table C-1.

TROUBLE
If Excel is not installed on your computer, Microsoft Graph opens and your screen will look different.

4. **Click OK**
   Excel opens in a split window sharing the screen with the PowerPoint window as shown in Figure C-10. The PowerPoint window displays the clustered column chart, and the Excel window displays sample data in a worksheet. The Chart Tools Design tab on the Ribbon contains commands you use in PowerPoint to work with the chart. The worksheet consists of rows and columns. The intersection of a row and a column is called a **cell**. Cells are referred to by their row and column location; for example, the cell at the intersection of column A and row 1 is called cell A1. Cells in the first or left column contain **axis labels** that identify the data in a row for example, "Category 1" is an axis label. Cells in the first or top row appear in the **legend** and describe the data in the series. Cells below and to the right of the axis labels and legend names contain the data values that are represented in the chart. Each column and row of data in the worksheet is called a **data series**. Each data series has corresponding **data series markers** in the chart, which are graphical representations such as bars, columns, or pie wedges. The gray boxes with the numbers along the left side of the worksheet are **row headings**, and the gray boxes with the letters along the top of the worksheet are **column headings**.

5. **Move the pointer over the worksheet in the Excel window**
   The pointer changes to ✛. Cell A6 is the **active cell**, which means that it is selected. The active cell has a thick black border around it.

6. **Click cell C4**
   Cell C4 is now the active cell.

7. **Click the Excel Window Close button ✕ on the title bar**
   The Excel window closes, and the PowerPoint window fills the screen. The new chart on the slide displays the data from the Excel worksheet.

8. **Click in a blank area of the slide to deselect the chart, then save your changes**
   The Chart Tools Design tab is no longer active.

FIGURE C-9: Insert Chart dialog box

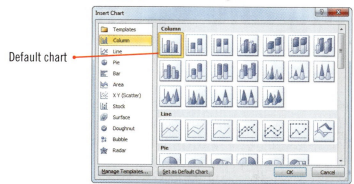

Default chart

FIGURE C-10: The PowerPoint and Excel split windows

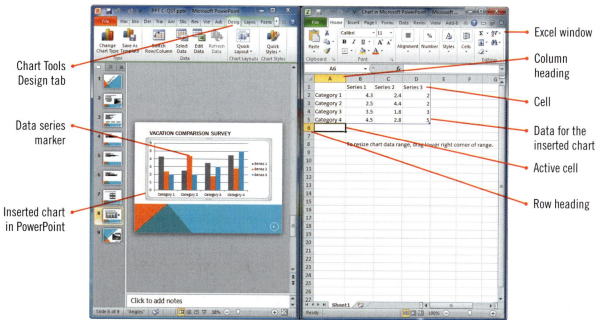

Chart Tools Design tab

Data series marker

Inserted chart in PowerPoint

Excel window

Column heading

Cell

Data for the inserted chart

Active cell

Row heading

TABLE C-1: Chart types

chart type	icon looks like	use to
Column		Track values over time or across categories
Line		Track values over time
Pie		Compare individual values to the whole
Bar		Compare values in categories or over time
Area		Show contribution of each data series to the total over time
XY (Scatter)		Compare pairs of values
Stock		Show stock market information or scientific data
Surface		Show value trends across two dimensions
Doughnut		Compare individual values to the whole with multiple series
Bubble		Indicate relative size of data points
Radar		Show changes in values in relation to a center point

Inserting Objects into a Presentation

Entering and Editing Chart Data

After you insert a chart into your presentation, you need to replace the sample data with the correct information. If you have data in an Excel worksheet or another source, you can import it from Excel; otherwise, you can type your own data into the worksheet. As you enter data and make other changes in the Excel worksheet, the chart in PowerPoint automatically reflects the new changes.  You enter and format survey data you collected that asked people to rate four categories of vacations with respect to three factors: price, safety, and culture.

1. **Click the chart on Slide 8, click the Chart Tools Design tab on the Ribbon, then click the Edit Data button in the Data group**

   The chart is selected in PowerPoint, and the worksheet opens in a separate Excel window. The data in the worksheet needs to be replaced with the correct information.

   > **QUICK TIP**
   > Click the chart in the PowerPoint window, then move your pointer over each bar in the chart to see the data source values.

2. **Click the Series 1 cell, type Price, press [Tab], type Safety, press [Tab], then type Culture**

   The Legend labels are entered. Pressing [Tab] in Excel moves the active cell from left to right one cell at a time in a row. Pressing [Enter] in the worksheet moves the active cell down one cell at a time in a column.

3. **Click the Category 1 cell, type Standard Rail, press [Enter], type Deluxe Rail, press [Enter], type Cruise, press [Enter], type Traditional, then press [Enter]**

   The axis labels are entered, and the chart in the PowerPoint window reflects all the changes.

4. **Enter the data shown in Figure C-11 to complete the worksheet, then press [Enter]**

   Column A needs to be wider to see all of the information in cell A2.

   > **QUICK TIP**
   > You can also drag a column divider line to resize the column width to accommodate the widest entry.

5. **Move ✛ over the column divider line between Column A and Column B, which changes to ↔, then double-click**

   Column A widens so you can see all of the data.

6. **Click the Switch Row/Column button in the Data group in the PowerPoint window**

   The data charted on the x-axis switches and moves to the y-axis. The y-axis is also referred to as the vertical axis or **value axis**, and the x-axis is also referred to as the horizontal axis or **category axis**. Notice the legend now displays the row axis labels instead of the column axis labels. You have finished entering the data in the Excel worksheet.

7. **Click the Excel window Close button ✕**

   Notice that the height of each column in the chart, as well as the values along the y-axis, adjust to reflect the numbers you typed. The column axis labels are now on the x-axis of the chart, and the row axis labels are listed in the legend.

8. **Click the More button ⊽ in the Chart Styles group, then click Style 26 (4th row)**

   The new chart style gives the column data markers a three-dimensional look.

9. **Click a blank area on the slide, then save the presentation**

   Compare your chart to Figure C-12.

FIGURE C-11: Worksheet showing chart data

	A	B	C	D	E	F	G
1		Price	Safety	Culture			
2	Standard Ra	63%	76%	54%			
3	Deluxe Rail	49%	84%	79%			
4	Cruise	57%	90%	41%			
5	Traditional	71%	56%	27%			
6							
7							
8		To resize chart data range, drag lower right corner of range.					

New chart data

Sheet1

FIGURE C-12: Formatted chart

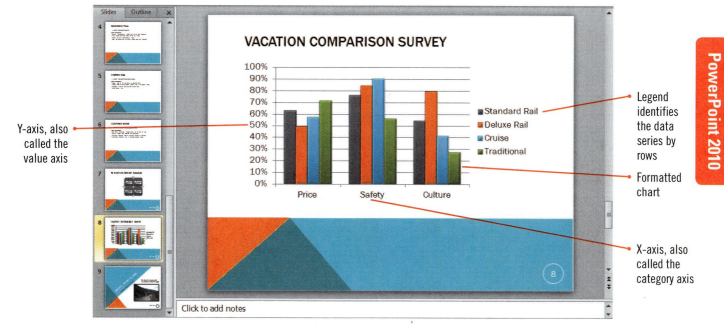

Y-axis, also called the value axis

Legend identifies the data series by rows

Formatted chart

X-axis, also called the category axis

Switching rows and columns

If you have difficulty visualizing what the Switch Row/Column command does, think about what is represented in the chart. **Series in Rows** means that the data in the datasheet rows is plotted on the y-axis, and the row axis labels are shown on the x-axis. The column axis labels are shown in the legend. **Series in Columns** means that the data in the datasheet columns is plotted on the y-axis, and the row axis labels are shown in the legend. The column axis labels are plotted on the x-axis.

Inserting a Table

As you create your presentation, you may have some information that would look best organized in rows and columns. For example, if you wanted to compare the basic details of three different cruise tours side by side, a table is ideal for this type of information. Once you have created a table, two new tabs, the Table Tools Design tab and the Table Tools Layout tab, appear on the Ribbon. You can use the Design tab to apply color styles, change cell borders, and add cell effects. Using the Layout tab, you can add rows and columns to your table, adjust the size of cells, and align text in the cells.  You decide that a table best illustrates the different services offered by the train tour company.

STEPS

QUICK TIP

You can also create a table by clicking the Table button in the Tables group on the Insert tab, then dragging ↳ over the table grid to create the size table you want.

1. **Right-click** Slide 7 **in the Slides tab, click** New Slide **on the shortcut menu, click the** title placeholder, **then type** Service Levels and Prices

   A new slide with the Title and Content layout appears.

2. **Click the** Insert Table icon ▦, **type** 4 **in the Number of columns text box, click the** Number of rows text box, **click the up arrow until** 5 **appears, then click** OK

   A formatted table with four columns and five rows appears on the slide, and the Table Tools Design tab opens on the Ribbon. The table has 20 cells. The insertion point is in the first cell of the table and is ready to accept text.

QUICK TIP

Press [Tab] when the insertion point is in the last cell of a table to create a new row.

3. **Type** Classic, **press** [Tab], **type** Deluxe, **press** [Tab], **type** Exclusive, **press** [Tab], **type** Royal, **then press** [Tab]

   The text you typed appears in the top four cells of the table. Pressing [Tab] moves the insertion point to the next cell; pressing [Enter] moves the insertion point to the next line in the same cell.

4. **Enter the rest of the table information shown in Figure C-13**

   The table would look better if it were formatted differently.

5. **Click the** More button ▾ **in the Table Styles group, scroll to the bottom of the gallery, then click** Medium Style 3 – Accent 2

   The background and text color change to reflect the table style you applied.

QUICK TIP

Change the height or width of any table cell by dragging its borders.

6. **Click the** upper-left cell, **click the** Table Tools Layout tab, **click the** Select button **in the Table group, click** Select Row, **then click the** Center button ▤ **in the Alignment group**

   The text in the top row is centered horizontally in each cell.

7. **Click the** Select button **in the Table group, click** Select Table, **then click the** Center Vertically button ▤ **in the Alignment group**

   The text in the whole table is centered vertically within each cell. The table would look better if all the rows were the same height.

8. **Click the** Distribute Rows button ▤ **in the Cell Size group, click the** Table Tools Design tab, **then click the** Effects button ▣▾ **in the Table Styles group**

   The Table Effects gallery opens.

9. **Point to** Cell Bevel, **click** Hard Edge **(3rd row), press** [Down arrow] **three times, click a blank area of the slide, then save the presentation**

   The 3-D effect makes the cells of the table stand out. The table looks better nudged away from the slide title. Compare your screen with Figure C-14.

FIGURE C-13: Inserted table with data

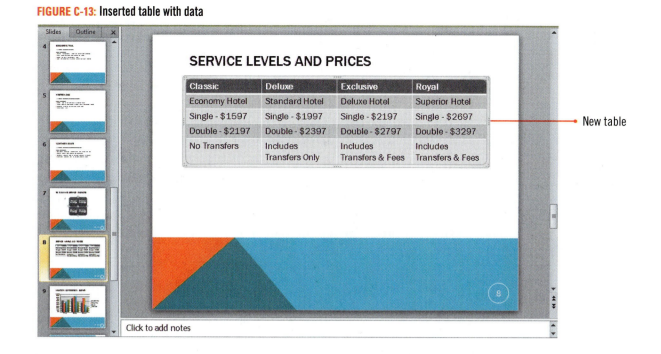

New table

FIGURE C-14: Formatted table

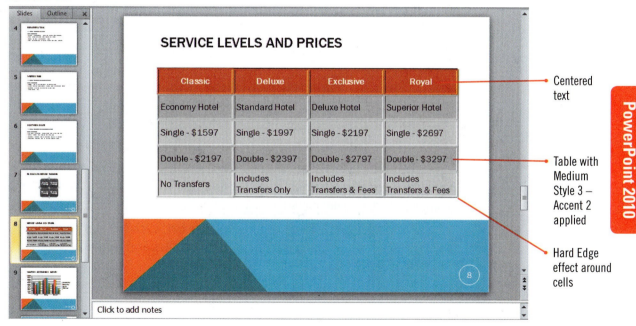

Centered text

Table with Medium Style 3 — Accent 2 applied

Hard Edge effect around cells

Drawing tables

Choose the slide where you want the table, click the Table button in the Tables group on the Insert tab, then click Draw Table. The pointer changes to ✎. Drag to define the boundaries of the table in the area of the slide where you want the table. A dotted outline appears as you draw. Next, you draw to create the rows and columns of your table. Click the Table Tools Design tab on the Ribbon, click the Draw Table button in the Draw Borders group, then draw lines for columns and rows. Be sure to draw within the boundary line of the table.

Inserting and Formatting WordArt

As you work to create an interesting presentation, your goal should include making your slides visually appealing. Sometimes plain text can come across as dull and unexciting in a presentation. **WordArt** is a set of decorative text styles, or text effects, that you can apply to any text object to help direct the attention of your audience to a certain piece of information. You can use WordArt in two different ways: you can apply a WordArt text style to an existing text object that converts the text into WordArt, or you can create a new WordArt object. The WordArt text styles and effects include text shadows, reflections, glows, bevels, 3-D rotations, and transformations. Use WordArt to create a new WordArt text object on Slide 3.

STEPS

QUICK TIP
You can format any text with a WordArt style. Select the text, click the Drawing Tools Format tab on the Ribbon, then click a WordArt style option in the WordArt Styles group.

1. Click the **Slide 3 thumbnail** in the Slides tab, click the **Insert tab** on the Ribbon, then click the **WordArt button** in the Text group

   The WordArt gallery appears displaying 30 WordArt text styles.

2. Click **Fill – Ice Blue, Text 2, Outline – Background 2,** (first style in the first row)

   A text object appears in the middle of the slide displaying sample text with the WordArt style you just selected.

3. Click the edge of the WordArt text object, then when the pointer changes to ⭧, drag the **text object** to the blank area of the slide

4. Click the **More button** ▾ in the WordArt Styles group, move your mouse over all of the WordArt styles in the gallery, then click **Fill – Orange, Accent 2, Warm Matte Bevel**

   The WordArt Styles change the sample text in the WordArt text object. The new WordArt style is applied to the text object.

5. Drag to select the text **Your text here** in the WordArt text object, click the **Decrease Font Size button** A▾ in the Mini toolbar until **40** appears in the Font Size text box, type **Guaranteed best**, press [Enter], then type **vacation in Canada**

   The text is smaller and appears on two lines.

6. Click the **Text Effects button** in the WordArt Styles group, point to **Transform**, click **Triangle Down** in the Warp section (first row), then click a blank area of the slide

   The transform effect is applied to the text object. Compare your screen to Figure C-15.

7. Click the **Reading View button** 📖 on the status bar, click the **Next button** ➡ until you reach Slide 10, click the **Menu button** 📑, then click **End Show**

8. Click the **Slide Sorter button** 🔲 on the status bar

   Compare your screen with Figure C-16.

9. Click the **Normal button** 📇 on the status bar, add your name as a footer to the notes and handouts, save your changes, submit your presentation to your instructor, then exit PowerPoint

FIGURE C-15: WordArt inserted on slide

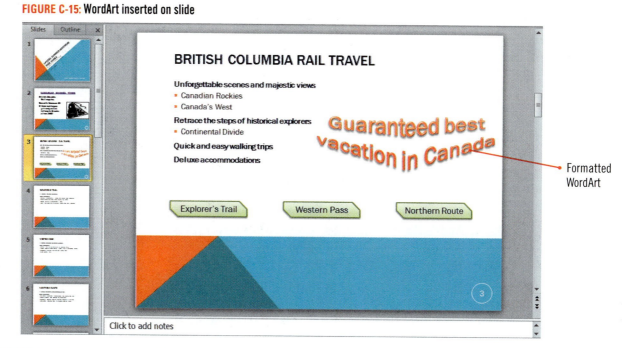

Formatted WordArt

FIGURE C-16: Completed presentation in Slide Sorter view

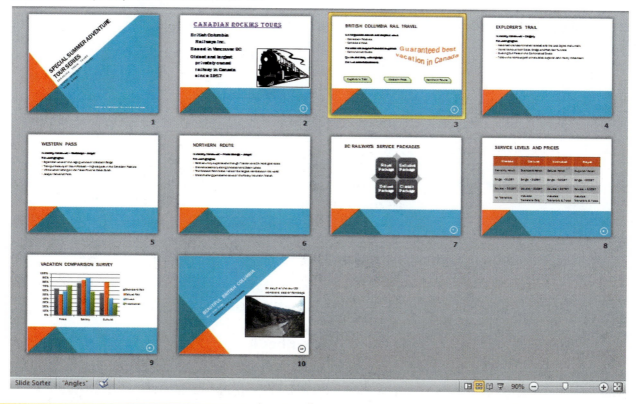

Saving a presentation as a video

You can save your PowerPoint presentation as a full-fidelity video, which incorporates all slide timings, transitions, animations, and narrations. The video can be distributed using a disc, the Web, or e-mail. Depending on how you want to display your video, you have three resolution settings from which to choose: Computer & HD Displays, Internet & DVD, and Portable Devices. The Large setting, Computer & HD Displays (960 × 720), is used for viewing on a computer monitor, projector, or other high definition displays. The Medium setting, Internet & DVD (640 × 480), is used for uploading to the Web or copying to a standard DVD. The Small setting, Portable Devices (320 × 240), is used on portable devices including portable media players such as Microsoft Zune. To save your presentation as a video, click the File tab, click Save & Send, click Create a Video, choose your settings, then click the Create Video button.

Practice

For current SAM information, including versions and content details, visit SAM Central (http://www.cengage.com/samcentral). If you have a SAM user profile, you may have access to hands-on instruction, practice, and assessment of the skills covered in this unit. Since various versions of SAM are supported throughout the life of this text, check with your instructor for the correct instructions and URL/Web site for accessing assignments.

Concepts Review

Label each element of the PowerPoint window shown in Figure C-17.

FIGURE C-17

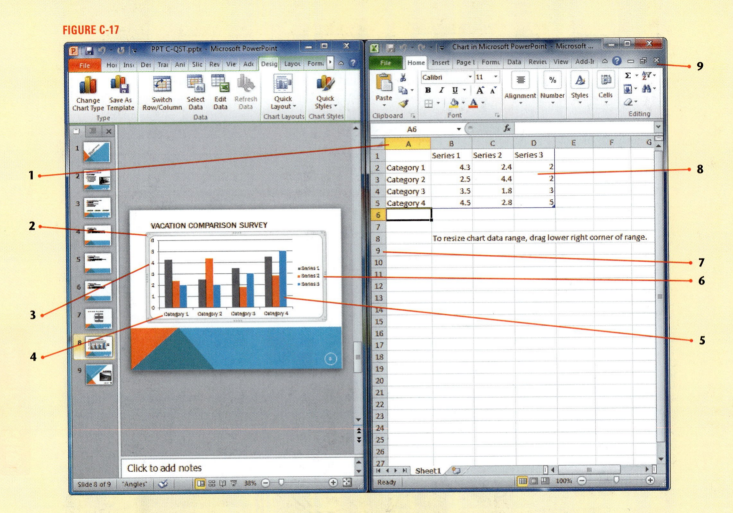

Match each term with the statement that best describes it.

10. Collection	a. Contains the numerical data displayed in a chart
11. Crop	b. The folder in the Clip Organizer that stores clip art
12. Worksheet	c. A presentation that is designed and formatted and usually comes with sample text
13. Table	d. PowerPoint object that compares data in columns and rows
14. Template	e. Hides a portion of a picture

Select the best answer from the list of choices.

15. What is the file index system that stores clip art, photographs, and movies called?
- **a.** Clip Art Index
- **b.** WordArt Gallery
- **c.** Microsoft Clip Organizer
- **d.** Office Media Collections

16. According to this unit, which media type is defined as line art or art work created in another program?
- **a.** Picture
- **b.** Clip art
- **c.** Video
- **d.** Animation

17. In PowerPoint, what is the graphical representation of data on a slide called?
- **a.** Table
- **b.** Worksheet
- **c.** Legend
- **d.** Chart

18. According to this unit, to compare data side by side, which of the following objects should you select?
- **a.** Table
- **b.** Chart
- **c.** Outline
- **d.** Grid

19. An object that has its own data source and becomes a part of your presentation after you insert it best describes which of the following?
- **a.** A Word outline
- **b.** An embedded object
- **c.** A WordArt object
- **d.** A table

20. A presentation designed and formatted with background elements, colors, and other graphic elements that you can use to create a new presentation is a _____.
- **a.** template
- **b.** theme
- **c.** video
- **d.** gallery

21. Use _____ to apply a set of decorative text styles or text effects to text.
- **a.** a template
- **b.** rich text format
- **c.** a collection
- **d.** WordArt

Skills Review

1. Insert text from Microsoft Word.
- **a.** Open the file PPT C-4.pptx from the drive and folder where you store your Data Files, then save it as **PPT C-Vista**. You will work to create the completed presentation as shown in Figure C-18.
- **b.** Click Slide 3 in the Slides tab, then use the Slides from Outline command to insert the file PPT C-5.docx from the drive and folder where you store your Data Files.
- **c.** In the Slides tab, drag Slide 5 above Slide 4.

FIGURE C-18

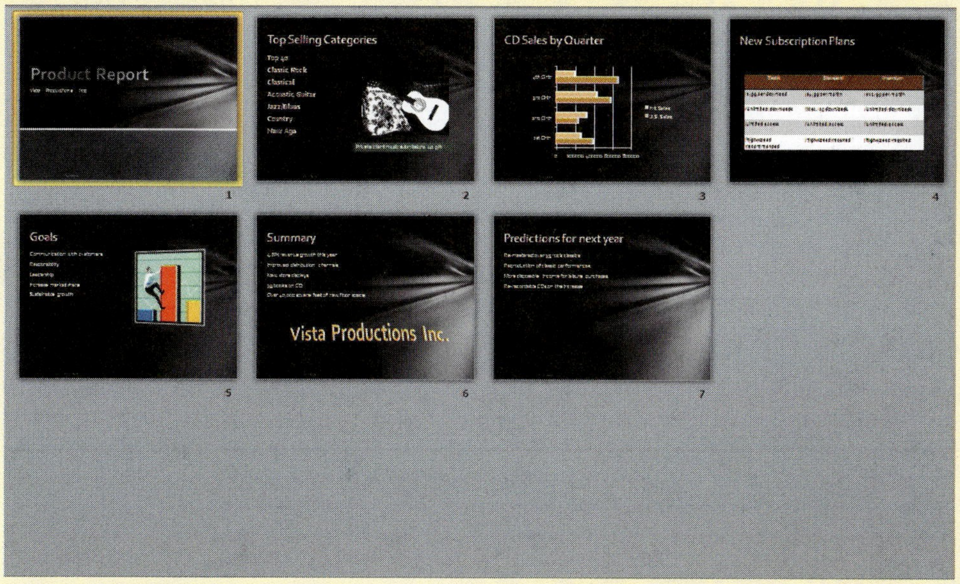

Skills Review (continued)

d. In the Slides tab, delete Slide 7, Expansion Potential.

e. Select Slides 4, 5, and 6 in the Slides tab, reset the slides to the default theme settings, then save your work.

2. **Insert clip art.**

a. Select Slide 4, then change the slide layout to the Two Content slide layout.

b. Press [Shift], click the text object, then change the font size to 18.

c. Click the clip art icon in the right content placeholder, search for clip art using the keywords **business goals**, insert the clip art shown in Figure C-18, then close the Clip Art task pane.

d. Click the Picture Border list arrow, change the color of the clip art border to White, Text 1.

e. Click the Picture Border list arrow, change the weight of the clip art border to 3 pt.

f. Click the Picture Effects button, point to 3-D Rotation, then click Perspective Left.

g. Drag the clip art so the top lines up with the top of the text object, then save your changes.

3. **Insert and style a picture.**

a. Select Slide 2, then insert the picture PPT C-6.jpg.

b. Completely crop the light blue section off the top of the picture, then crop the right side of the picture about $1/4$ inch.

c. Drag the picture up so it is in the center of the blank area of the slide.

d. Click the Color button, then change the picture color to Black and White: 25%.

e. Save your changes.

4. **Insert a text box.**

a. On Slide 2, insert a text box below the picture.

b. Type **Private client submissions for music up 9%**.

c. Delete the word **for**, then drag the word **music** after the word **client**.

d. Select the text object, then click the More button in the Shape Styles group on the Drawing Tools Format tab.

e. Click Intense Effect – Green, Accent 6.

f. Center the text object under the picture.

5. **Insert a chart.**

a. Go to Slide 3, CD Sales by Quarter, click the Insert tab on the ribbon, click the Chart button in the Illustrations group, then insert a Clustered Bar chart.

b. Close Excel.

6. **Enter and edit chart data.**

a. Show the chart data.

b. Enter the data shown in Table C-2 into the worksheet.

c. Delete the data in each cell in Column D, then close Excel.

d. Change the chart style to Style 12 in the Chart Styles group.

e. Move the chart to the center of the blank area of the slide, then save your changes.

TABLE C-2

	U.S. Sales	Int. Sales
1st Qtr	390,957	263,902
2nd Qtr	229,840	325,854
3rd Qtr	585,063	435,927
4th Qtr	665,113	203,750

7. **Insert a table.**

a. Add a new slide after Slide 3 with the Title and Content layout.

b. Add the slide title **New Subscription Plans**.

c. Insert a table with three columns and five rows.

d. Enter the information shown in Table C-3, then change the table style to Medium Style 3 – Accent 3. (*Hint*: Use the Copy and Paste commands to enter duplicate information in the table.)

e. Center the text in the top row.

f. In the Table Tools Layout tab, distribute the table rows.

g. Move the table to the center of the blank area of the slide, then save your changes.

TABLE C-3

Basic	Standard	Premium
$.99 per download	$4.99 per month	$12.95 per month
Unlimited downloads	Max. 25 downloads	Unlimited downloads
Limited access	Unlimited access	Unlimited access
High-speed recommended	High-speed required	High-speed required

Skills Review (continued)

8. **Insert and format WordArt.**

   a. Go to Slide 6, then, insert a WordArt text object using the Fill – Brown, Accent 3, Outline – Text 2 style.

   b. Type **Vista Productions Inc.**, then apply the WordArt style Fill – Gold, Accent 2, Warm Matte Bevel.

   c. Apply the Inflate Top Transform effect (seventh row) to the text object, then move the text object to the middle of the blank area of the slide.

   d. View the presentation in Slide Show view, then check the spelling of the presentation.

   e. Add your name as a footer to all the slides, then save your changes.

   f. Submit your presentation to your instructor, close your presentation, and exit PowerPoint.

Independent Challenge 1

You are a financial management consultant for Goodrich & Young Investments LLP, located in Syracuse, New York. One of your responsibilities is to create standardized presentations on different financial investments for use on the company Web site. As part of the presentation for this meeting, you insert some clip art, add a text box, and insert a chart.

If you have a SAM 2010 user profile, an autogradable SAM version of this assignment may be available at http://www.cengage.com/sam2010. Check with your instructor to confirm that this assignment is available in SAM. To use the SAM version of this assignment, log into the SAM 2010 Web site and download the instruction and start files.

   a. Open the file PPT C-7.pptx from the drive and folder where you store your Data Files, then save it as **PPT C-Goodrich**.

   b. Add your name as the footer on all of the slides, then apply the Horizon Design Theme.

   c. Insert a clustered column chart on Slide 6, then enter the data in Table C-4 into the worksheet. Delete the unwanted placeholder data in the chart.

   d. Format the chart using Style 35, then move the chart down slightly away from the title text object.

TABLE C-4

	1 year	3 year	5 year	7 year
Bonds	2.2%	3.2%	3.9%	4.5%
Stocks	1.9%	2.2%	4.2%	3.6%
Mutual Funds	2.6%	4.0%	8.4%	6.4%

Advanced Challenge Exercise

   ■ Click the Chart Tools Layout tab, click the Legend button, then click Show Legend at Top.

   ■ Click the Chart Tools Format tab, then click the Chart Elements list arrow in the Current Selection group, then click Series "3 year."

   ■ Click the Shape Fill list arrow in the Shape Styles group, then click Gold, Text 2, under Theme Colors.

   e. Insert clip art of a set of balance scales on Slide 2, then position and format as necessary. (*Hint*: Use the keyword **balance scales** to search for clips.)

   f. On Slide 3, use the Align command and Distribute command on the Drawing Tools Format tab in the Arrange group to align and distribute the objects so that the shapes are aligned on top and distributed horizontally.

   g. Check the spelling of the presentation, view the slide show, make any necessary changes, then save your work. See Figure C-19.

   h. Submit the presentation to your instructor, then close the presentation, and exit PowerPoint.

FIGURE C-19

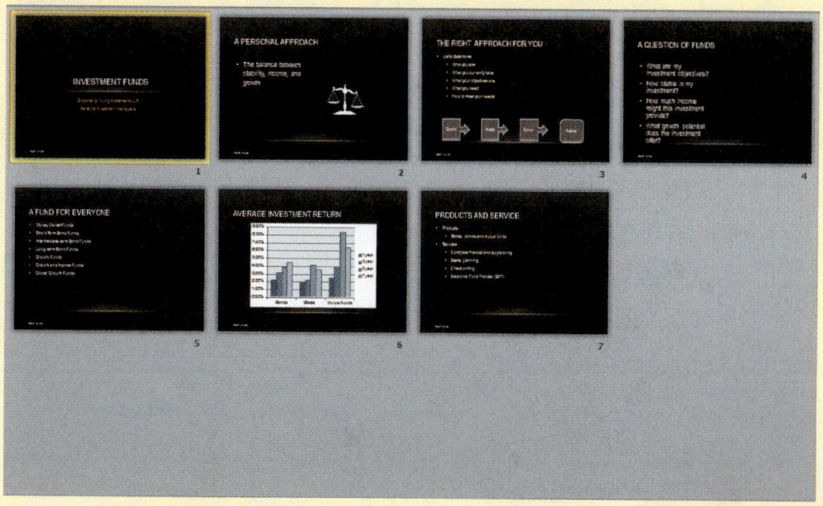

Independent Challenge 2

You work for Veil Home Systems, a company based in Michigan that provides integrated data, security, and voice command systems for homes. You have been asked to enhance a marketing presentation on a new product that the company is going to promote at a large trade fair in Las Vegas. You work on completing a presentation for the show. You insert some clip art, add a text box, and insert a chart.

a. Start PowerPoint, open the file PPT C-8.pptx from the drive and folder where you store your Data Files, and save it as **PPT C-Veil**.

b. Add your name and today's date to Slide 1 in the Subtitle text box.

c. Organize the objects on Slide 2 using the Align, Distribute, and Group commands. Add and format additional shapes to enhance the presentation.

d. On Slide 3, style the picture, recolor the picture, and use a picture effect.

e. Apply the Hardcover theme to the presentation.

f. Insert the Word document file PPT C-9.docx to create additional slides from an outline after Slide 2.

g. Select Slides 3 and 4, then reset the slides to their default settings.

h. Create a new slide after Slide 4, title the slide **Growth of Integrated Systems**, then insert a chart.

i. Enter the data in Table C-5, then format the chart using at least two formatting commands. Be able to name which formatting commands you applied to the chart.

TABLE C-5

	Last Yr.	Current Yr.	Next Yr.
Traditional	73	94	103
Integrated	15	36	55

j. Insert a text box on the Veil Home Systems slide (Slide 7). Create your own company contact and address information. Format the text box.

k. Check the spelling, then view the final slide show (refer to Figure C-20). Make any necessary changes.

l. Save the presentation, submit the presentation to your instructor, close the file, and exit PowerPoint.

FIGURE C-20

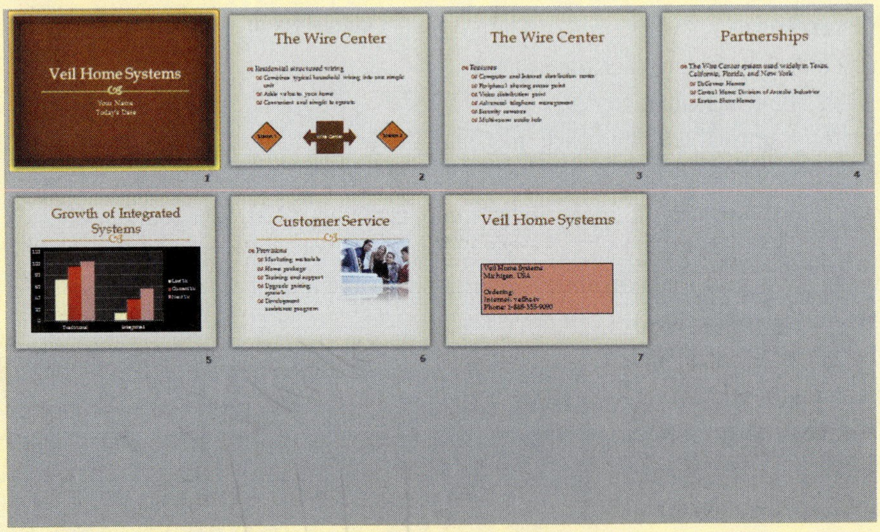

Independent Challenge 3

You work for LearnRight Inc. a company that produces instructional software to help people learn foreign languages. Once a year, LearnRight holds a meeting with their biggest client, the Department of State, to brief the government on new products and to receive feedback on existing products. Your boss has started a presentation and has asked you to look it over and add other elements to make it look better.

a. Start PowerPoint, open the file PPT C-10.pptx from the drive and folder where you store your Data Files, and save it as **PPT C-LearnRight**.

Independent Challenge 3 (continued)

b. Add an appropriate design theme to the presentation.

c. Insert the Word outline PPT C-11.docx after the Product Revisions slide, then reset Slides 5, 6, and 7 to the default settings.

d. Format the text so that the most important information is the most prominent.

e. Insert an appropriate table on a slide of your choice. Use your own information, or use text from a bulleted list on one of the slides.

f. Add at least two appropriate shapes that emphasize slide content. Format the objects using shape styles. If appropriate, use the Align, Distribute, and Group commands to organize your shapes.

Advanced Challenge Exercise (*Internet connection required*)

- Select a slide on which you want to add a clip art image. Open the Clip Art task pane, then click the Find more at Office.com link to go to the Office.com Web site.
- Download and insert an appropriate media clip from the Academic category. (*Hint*: Make sure you know the media clip's keywords; it will make searching for it in the Clip art task pane much easier.)
- Format the clip using Picture Tools Format tab.
- Be ready to explain how you formatted the clip.

g. Check the spelling and view the final slide show. Make any necessary changes.

h. Add your name as footer text on the notes and handouts, then save the presentation.

i. Submit your presentation to your instructor, close the file, then exit PowerPoint.

Real Life Independent Challenge

You are on the Foreign Exchange Commission at your college, and one of your responsibilities is to present information on past foreign student exchanges to different organizations on and off campus. You need to create a pictorial presentation that highlights a trip to a different country. Create a presentation using your own pictures or pictures given to you with permission by a friend.

Note: Three photographs (PPT C-12.jpg, PPT C-13.jpg, and PPT C-14.jpg) from Dijon, France, are provided to help you complete this Independent Challenge. You can use the provided photos if you have none of your own to use.

a. Start PowerPoint, create a new blank presentation, and save it as **PPT C-Exchange** to the drive and folder where you store your Data Files.

b. Locate and insert the pictures you want to use. Place one picture on each slide using the Content with Caption slide layout.

c. Add information about each picture in the text placeholder, and enter a slide title. If you use the pictures provided, research Dijon, France, using the Internet for relevant information to place on the slides (*Internet connection required*).

d. Apply an appropriate design theme, then apply an appropriate title and your name to the title slide.

e. Check the spelling, then view the final slide show (refer to Figure C-21).

f. Add a slide number and your class name as footer text to all of the slides, save your work, then submit your presentation to your instructor.

g. Close the file, and exit PowerPoint.

FIGURE C-21

Visual Workshop

Create a one-slide presentation that looks like Figure C-22. The slide layout shown in Figure C-22 is a specific layout designed for pictures. Insert the picture file PPT C-15.jpg to complete this presentation. Add your name as footer text to the slide, save the presentation as **PPT C-Guide** to the drive and folder where you store your Data Files, check the spelling of the presentation, then submit your presentation to your instructor.

FIGURE C-22

Finishing a Presentation

Files You Will Need:

PPT D-1.pptx
PPT D-2.jpg
PPT D-3.pptx
PPT D-4.jpg
PPT D-5.pptx
PPT D-6.pptx
PPT D-7.pptx

Though not required, having a consistent professional-looking theme throughout your presentation is best if you want to gain and retain your audience's interest in the subject you are presenting. PowerPoint helps you achieve a consistent look by providing ways to customize your slides' layout and background. Once you are finished working with the text and other objects of your presentation, you are ready to apply slide show effects, which determine the way the slides and objects on the slides appear in Slide Show view. You have reviewed the presentation and are pleased with the slides you created for the Quest Specialty Travel presentation. Now you are ready to finalize the look of the slides and add effects to make the presentation interesting to watch.

OBJECTIVES

Modify masters

Customize the background and theme

Use slide show commands

Set slide transitions and timings

Animate objects

Inspect a presentation

Evaluate a presentation

Create a template

Modifying Masters

Each presentation in PowerPoint has a set of **masters** that store information about the theme and slide layouts, including the position and size of text and content placeholders, fonts, slide background, color, and effects. There are three Master views: Slide Master view, Notes Master view, and Handout Master view. Changes made in Slide Master view are reflected on the slides in Normal view; changes made in Notes Master view are reflected in Notes Page view, and changes made in Handout Master view appear when you print your presentation using a handout printing option. The primary benefit to modifying a master is that you can make universal changes to your whole presentation instead of making individual repetitive changes to each of your slides. You want to add the QST company logo to every slide in your presentation, so you open your presentation and insert the logo to the slide master.

STEPS

1. **Start PowerPoint, open the presentation PPT D-1.pptx from the drive and folder where you store your Data Files, save the presentation as PPT D-QST, then click the View tab on the Ribbon**

   The title slide of the presentation appears.

   QUICK TIP
   You can press and hold [Shift] and click the Normal button on the status bar to display the slide master.

2. **Click the Slide Master button in the Master Views group, scroll to the top of the slide thumbnail pane, then click the Angles Slide Master thumbnail (first thumbnail)**

   A new tab, the Slide Master tab, appears next to the Home tab on the Ribbon. The Slide Master view appears with the slide master displayed in the Slide pane as shown in Figure D-1. The slide master is the theme slide master (the Angles theme in this case). Each theme comes with its own associated slide masters. Each master text placeholder on the slide master identifies the font size, style, color, and position of text placeholders on the slides in Normal view. For example, the Master title placeholder positioned at the top of the slide uses a black, 28 pt, uppercase, Franklin Gothic Medium font. Slide titles use this font style and formatting. Design elements that you place on the slide master appear on every slide in the presentation. The slide layouts located below the slide master in the slide thumbnail pane follow the information on the slide master. All changes you make to the slide master, including font changes, are reflected in all of the slide layouts.

   QUICK TIP
   When working with slide layouts, you can right-click the thumbnail to open a shortcut list of commands.

3. **Point to the slide layouts in the slide thumbnail pane, then click the Two Content Layout thumbnail**

   As you point to each slide layout, a ScreenTip appears identifying each slide layout by name and lists if any slides in the presentation are using the layout. Slides 2, 5, 7, and 9 are using the Two Content Layout.

4. **Click the Angles Slide Master thumbnail (first thumbnail), click the Insert tab on the Ribbon, then click the Picture button in the Images group**

   The Insert Picture dialog box opens.

5. **Select the picture file PPT D-2.jpg from the drive and folder where you store your Data Files, then click Insert**

   The QST graphic logo appears on the slide master and will appear on all slides in the presentation. The graphic is too large and needs to be repositioned on the slide.

6. **Click 1.61" in the Shape Width text box in the Size group, type 1, press [Enter], drag the graphic to the upper-left corner of the slide, then click a blank area of the slide**

   The graphic snaps into the corner of the slide.

7. **Click the Slide Master tab on the Ribbon, then click the Preserve button in the Edit Master group**

   Preserving the selected master assures that the Angles slide master remains with this presentation even if you eventually use another master. Compare your screen to Figure D-2.

8. **Click the Normal button [image] on the status bar, then save your changes**

FIGURE D-1: Slide Master view

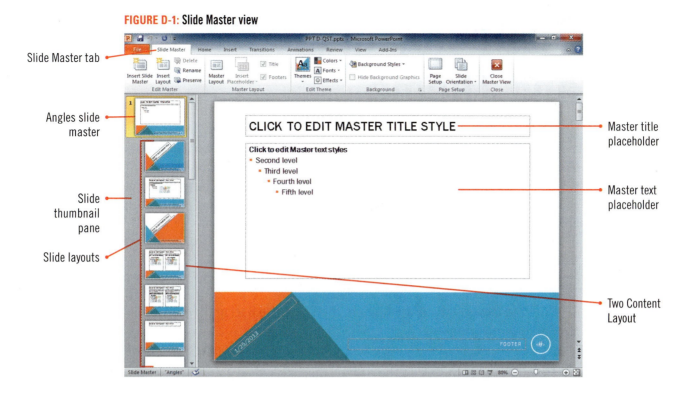

Slide Master tab

Angles slide master

Slide thumbnail pane

Slide layouts

Master title placeholder

Master text placeholder

Two Content Layout

FIGURE D-2: Graphic added to slide master

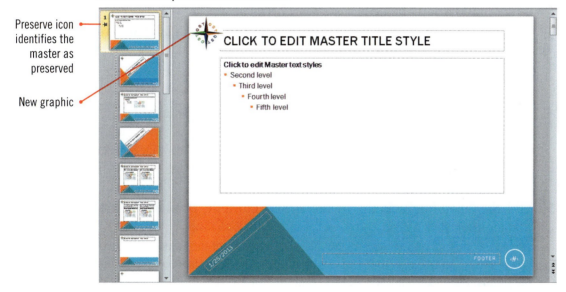

Preserve icon identifies the master as preserved

New graphic

Create custom slide layouts

As you work with PowerPoint, you may find that you need to develop a customized slide layout. For example, you may need to create presentations for a client that has slides that display four pictures with a caption underneath each picture. To make everyone's job easier, you can create a custom slide layout that includes only the placeholders that you need. To create a custom slide layout, open Slide Master view, and then click the Insert Layout button in the Edit Master group. A new slide layout appears in the slide thumbnail pane. You can choose to add several different

placeholders including Content, Text, Picture, Chart, Table, SmartArt, Media, and Clip Art. Click the Insert Placeholder list arrow in the Master Layout group, click the placeholder you want to add, drag ✛ to create the placeholder, then position the placeholder on the slide. In Slide Master view, you can add or delete placeholders in any of the slide layouts. You can rename a custom slide layout by clicking the Rename button in the Edit Master group and entering a descriptive name to better identify the layout.

PowerPoint 2010

Finishing a Presentation

PowerPoint 75

Customizing the Background and Theme

Every slide in a PowerPoint presentation has a **background**, the area behind the text and graphics. You modify the background to enhance the slides using images and color. A **background graphic** is an object placed on the slide master. You can quickly change the background appearance by applying a background style, which is a set of color variations derived from the theme colors. Theme colors determine the colors for all slide elements in your presentation, including slide background, text and lines, shadows, fills, accents, and hyperlinks. Every PowerPoint theme has its own set of theme colors. See Table D-1 for a description of the theme colors. The QST presentation needs some design enhancements. You decide to modify the background of the slides by changing the theme colors and fonts.

STEPS

1. **Click the Design tab on the Ribbon, then click the Background Styles button in the Background group**

   A gallery of background styles opens. Review the different backgrounds using Live Preview.

QUICK TIP

To apply a new background style to only selected slides, select the slides on the Slides tab or in Slide Sorter view, right-click the background style in the Background Styles gallery, then click Apply to Selected Slides.

2. **Move ⬉ over each style in the gallery, then click Style 2**

   Figure D-3 shows the new background on Slide 1 of the presentation and the other slides in the Slides tab. Even though you are working in Normal view, the new background style is applied to the slide master and slide layouts. The new background style does not appear over the whole slide, which indicates there are background items on the slide master preventing you from seeing the entire slide background.

3. **Click the Slide 2 thumbnail in the Slides tab, then click the Hide Background Graphics check box in the Background group**

   All of the background items (the QST graphic and colored shapes at the bottom of the slide) are hidden from view, and only the text objects, slide number, and train clip remain visible.

4. **Click the Hide Background Graphics check box, click the Background Styles button in the Background group, then click Style 1**

   All of the background items and the white background appear again. The white background color you started with actually looks the best. Theme colors that better match the QST logo would look better than the current theme colors.

QUICK TIP

To create custom theme colors, click the Colors button, then click Create New Theme Colors. You can also create custom theme fonts by clicking the Fonts button, then clicking Create New Theme Fonts.

5. **Click the Colors button in the Themes group, move the pointer over each of the built-in themes, then click Aspect**

   The new theme colors are applied to the slide master and all of the elements in the presentation including background items, tables, the SmartArt graphic on Slide 4, and the chart on Slide 11. Notice the title text font, color, and formatting did not change; this is known as an **exception**. Exceptions are changes that you make directly to text on the slide, which do not match the theme fonts on the slide master.

6. **Click the Slide 4 thumbnail in the Slides tab, click the Effects button in the Themes group, move the pointer over each of the built-in themes, then click Elemental**

   Notice how the new theme effects change the SmartArt graphic. Like the theme colors, the new theme effects are applied to the slide master and to all of the slides in the presentation.

7. **Click the Slide 5 thumbnail in the Slides tab, click the Fonts button in the Themes group, move the pointer over each of the built-in themes, click Composite, then save your work**

   The new theme fonts are applied to the presentation. Compare your screen to Figure D-4.

FIGURE D-3: Slide with new background style applied

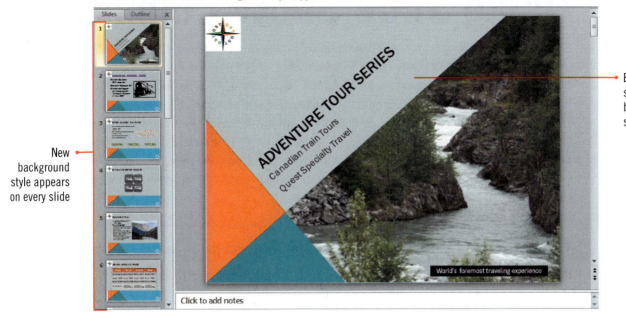

New background style appears on every slide

Background style appears behind all slide objects

FIGURE D-4: Slide showing new theme colors and theme fonts

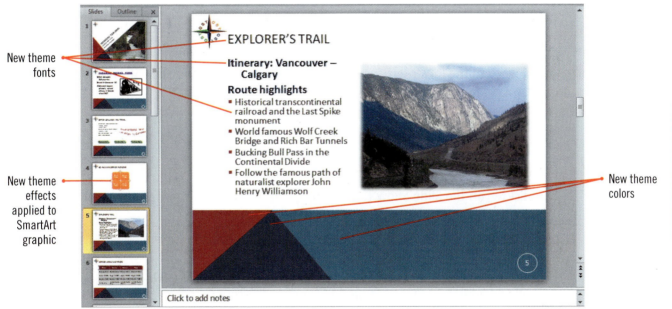

New theme fonts

New theme effects applied to SmartArt graphic

New theme colors

TABLE D-1: Theme colors

color element	description
Text/Background colors	Contrasting colors for typed characters and the slide background
Accent colors	There are six accent colors used for shapes, drawn lines, and text; the shadow color for text and objects and the fill and outline color for shapes are all accent colors; all of these colors contrast appropriately with background and text colors
Hyperlink color	Colors used for hyperlinks you insert
Followed Hyperlink color	Color used for hyperlinks after they have been clicked

Using Slide Show Commands

With PowerPoint, you can show a presentation on a computer using Slide Show view. Slide Show view is used primarily to deliver a presentation to an audience, either over the Internet using your computer or through a projector connected to your computer. As you've seen, Slide Show view fills your computer screen with the slides of the presentation, showing them one at a time. Once the presentation is in Slide Show view, you can use a number of slide show options to tailor the show to meet your needs. For example, you can draw, or **annotate**, on slides or jump to different slides in other parts of the presentation. 🎨 You want to learn how to run a slide show and use the slide show options so you will be prepared when you give your presentation. You run the slide show of the presentation and practice using some of the custom slide show options.

1. **Click the Slide 1 thumbnail in the Slides tab, then click the Slide Show button 🖵 on the status bar**

   The first slide of the presentation fills the screen.

2. **Press [Spacebar]**

   Slide 2 appears on the screen. Pressing [Spacebar] or clicking the left mouse button is the easiest way to move through a slide show. See Table D-2 for other Slide Show view keyboard commands. You can also use the Slide Show shortcut menu for on-screen navigation during a slide show.

   > **QUICK TIP**
   > During a slide show you can also type the slide number, then press [Enter] to jump to a slide.

3. **Right-click anywhere on the screen, point to Go to Slide on the shortcut menu, then click 7 Western Pass**

   The slide show jumps to Slide 7. You can highlight or emphasize major points in your presentation by annotating the slide during a slide show using one of PowerPoint's annotation tools.

   > **TROUBLE**
   > The Slide Show toolbar buttons are semitransparent and blend in with the background color on the slide.

4. **Move ⓡ to the lower-left corner of the screen to display the Slide Show toolbar, click the Pen Options menu button ✐, then click Highlighter**

   The pointer changes to the highlighter pointer ▮.

5. **Drag ▮ to highlight the text in the first and fourth bullet points on the slide**

   While the annotation tool is visible, mouse clicks do not advance the slide show; however, you can still move to the next slide by pressing [Spacebar] or [Enter].

6. **Click ✐ on the Slide Show toolbar, click Pen, draw a circle around the train tunnel in the picture, then press [Esc]**

   Pressing [Esc] or [Ctrl][A] while using an annotation pointer (pen pointer or highlighter pointer) switches the pointer back to ⓡ. Compare your screen to Figure D-5.

7. **Click ✐ on the Slide Show toolbar, click Eraser, the pointer changes to ⬚, then click the yellow highlight annotation on the fourth bullet point**

   The annotation is erased.

8. **Press [Esc], click ✐, then click Erase All Ink on Slide**

   The annotations on Slide 7 are erased. You also have the option of saving annotations you don't delete in Slide Show view when you quit the slide show. Saved annotations appear as drawn objects in Normal view.

   > **QUICK TIP**
   > To temporarily hide your slide during a slide show, right-click the screen, point to Screen, then click Black Screen or White Screen.

9. **Click the Slide Show menu button 🔲 on the Slide Show toolbar, point to Go to Slide, then click 1 Adventure Tour Series on the menu**

   Slide 1 appears.

10. **Press [Enter] to advance through the slide show, then when you see a black slide, press [Spacebar]**

    The black slide indicates the end of the slide show, and you are returned to Slide 1 in Normal view.

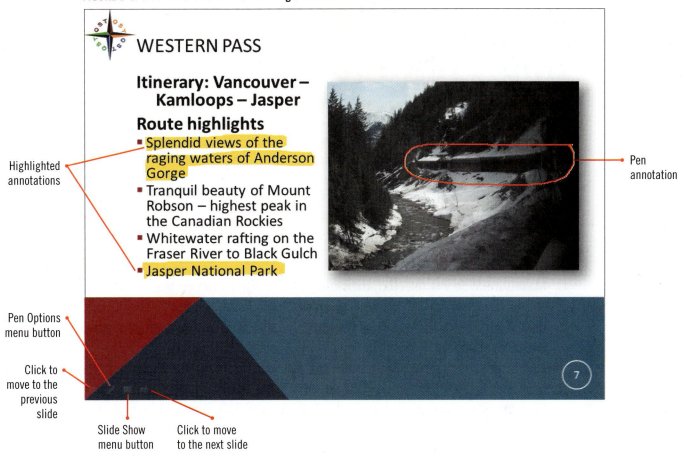

Highlighted annotations

Pen annotation

Pen Options menu button

Click to move to the previous slide

Slide Show menu button

Click to move to the next slide

TABLE D-2: Basic slide show keyboard commands

keyboard commands	description
[Enter], [Spacebar], [PgDn], [N], [down arrow], or [right arrow]	Advances to the next slide
[E]	Erases the annotation drawing
[Home], [End]	Moves to the first or last slide in the slide show
[H]	Displays a hidden slide
[up arrow] or [PgUp]	Returns to the previous slide
[W]	Changes the screen to white; press again to return
[S]	Pauses the slide show; press again to continue
[B]	Changes the screen to black; press again to return
[Ctrl][M]	Shows or hides annotations on the slide
[Ctrl][A]	Changes pointer to ⌖
[Esc]	Stops the slide show

Setting Slide Transitions and Timings

In a slide show, you can specify how each slide advances in and out of view, and for how long each slide appears on the screen. **Slide transitions** are the special visual and audio effects you apply to a slide that determine how it moves on and off the screen during the slide show. **Slide timing** refers to the amount of time a slide is visible on the screen. Typically, you only set slide timings if you want the presentation to automatically progress through the slides during a slide show. Setting the correct slide timing, in this case, is important because it determines how much time your audience has to view each slide. Each slide can have a different slide timing. You decide to set slide transitions and seven-second slide timings for all the slides.

STEPS

1. **Make sure Slide 1 is selected, then click the Transitions tab on the Ribbon**

   Transitions are organized by type into three groups.

2. **Click the More button** ⊡ **in the Transition to This Slide group, then click Glitter in the Exciting section**

   The new slide transition plays on the slide, and a transition icon ⭐ appears next to the slide thumbnail in the Slides tab as shown in Figure D-6. You can customize the slide transition by changing its direction and speed.

QUICK TIP
You can add a sound that plays with the transition from the Sound list arrow in the Timing group.

3. **Click the Effect Options button in the Transition to This Slide group, click Diamonds from Top, click the Duration down arrow in the Timing group until 2.00 appears, then click the Preview button in the Preview group**

   The Glitter slide transition now plays from the top of the slide for 2.00 seconds. You can apply this transition with the custom settings to all of the slides in the presentation.

4. **Click the Apply To All button in the Timing group, then click the Slide Sorter button** 🔠 **on the status bar**

   All of the slides now have the customized Glitter transition applied to them as identified by the transition icons located below each slide. You also have the ability to determine how slides progress during a slide show—either manually by mouse click or automatically by slide timing.

5. **Click the On Mouse Click check box under Advance Slide in the Timing group to clear the check mark**

   This clears the option that manually advances slides during a slide show. You can set both manual and automatic slide timings within the same presentation, which is why you need to clear the manual option. Now you can set an automatic slide timing.

QUICK TIP
Click the transition icon under any slide in Slide Sorter view to see its transition play.

6. **Click the After up arrow until 00:07.00 appears in the text box, then click the Apply To All button**

   The timing between slides is 7 seconds as indicated by the time under each slide in Slide Sorter view. See Figure D-7. When you run the slide show, each slide will remain on the screen for 7 seconds. You can override a slide's timing and speed up the slide show by pressing [Spacebar], [Enter], or clicking the left mouse button.

7. **Click the Slide Show button** 🖵 **on the status bar, then watch the slide show advance automatically**

8. **When you see the black slide at the end of the slide show, press [Spacebar], then save your changes**

   The slide show ends and returns to Slide Sorter view with Slide 1 selected.

FIGURE D-6: Applied slide transition

Transition icon

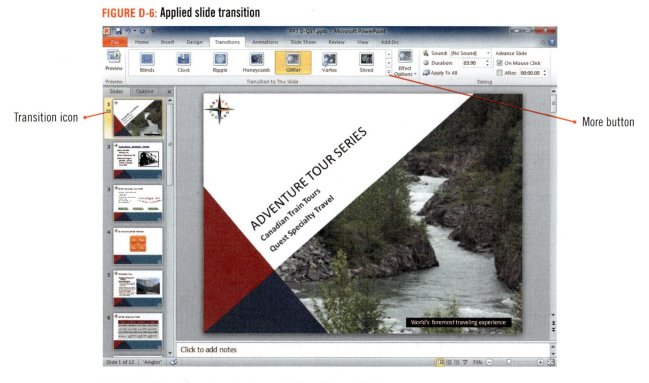

More button

FIGURE D-7: Slide Sorter view showing applied transition and timing

Transition icon

Slide timing

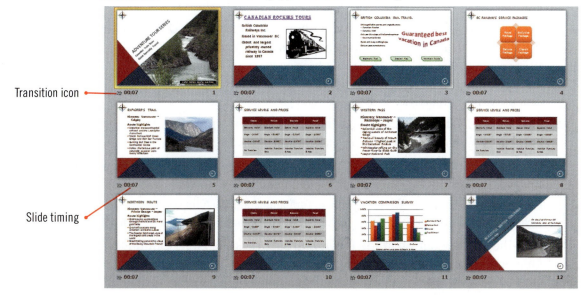

Rehearsing slide show timings

You can set different slide timings for each slide. For example, you can have the title slide appear for 20 seconds, the second slide for 1 minute, and so on. You can set timings by clicking the Rehearse Timings button in the Set Up group on the Slide Show tab. Slide Show view opens and the Recording toolbar shown in Figure D-8 opens. It contains buttons to pause between slides and to advance to the next slide. After opening the Recording toolbar, practice giving your presentation. PowerPoint keeps track of how long each slide appears and sets the timing accordingly. When you are finished rehearsing, PowerPoint displays the total recorded time for the presentation. The next time you run the slide show, you can use the timings you rehearsed.

FIGURE D-8: Recording toolbar

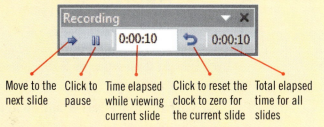

Move to the next slide

Click to pause

Time elapsed while viewing current slide

Click to reset the clock to zero for the current slide

Total elapsed time for all slides

Animating Objects

Animations let you control how objects and text appear on the screen during a slide show and allow you to manage the flow of information and emphasize specific facts. You can animate text, pictures, sounds, hyperlinks, SmartArt diagrams, charts, and individual chart elements. For example, you can apply a Fade animation to bulleted text so that each paragraph enters the slide separately from the others. Animations are organized into four categories, Entrance, Emphasis, Exit, and Motion Paths. The Entrance and Exit animations cause an object to enter or exit the slide with an effect. An Emphasis animation causes an object visible on the slide to have an effect and a Motion Path animation causes an object to move on a specified path on the slide. You animate the text and graphics of several slides in the presentation.

STEPS

1. **Double-click the Slide 1 thumbnail to return to Normal view, click the Animations tab on the Ribbon, then click the river picture**

   Text as well as other objects, like a picture, can be animated during a slide show.

   > **QUICK TIP**
   > There are additional animation options for each animation category located at the bottom of the animations gallery.

2. **Click the More button � in the Animation group, point to each of the animation options in the gallery, then click Shape in the Entrance section**

   As you point to each animation option a Live Preview of the effect plays. Animations can be serious and business-like or humorous, so be sure to choose appropriate effects for your presentation. A small numeral 1, called an animation tag 【1】, appears at the top corner of the picture. **Animation tags** identify the order in which objects are animated during slide show.

3. **Click the Effect Options button in the Animation group, click Diamond, then click the Duration up arrow in the Timing group until 04.00 appears**

   Effect options change for each animation. Changing the shape of the animation to diamond complements the shape of the picture, and increasing the duration of the animation gives it a more dramatic effect. Compare your screen to Figure D-9.

4. **Click the Slide Show button ☴ on the status bar, then press [Esc] when you see Slide 3**

   The Shape animation, with the Diamond effect, which begins after the slide transition, is active on Slide 1.

5. **On Slide 3, click the bulleted list text object, click ☴ in the Animation group, then click Grow & Turn in the Entrance section**

   The text object is animated with the Grow & Turn animation. Each line of text has an animation tag with each paragraph displaying a different number. Accordingly, each paragraph is animated separately.

6. **Click the Preview button in the Preview group, click the Effect Options button in the Animation group, click All at Once, then click the Duration up arrow in the Timing group until 02.50 appears**

   Notice that the animation tags for each line of text in the text object now have the same numeral (1), indicating that each line of text animates at the same time.

   > **QUICK TIP**
   > If you want to individually animate the parts of a grouped object, then you must ungroup the objects before you animate them.

7. **Press [Shift], click the shapes object at the bottom of the slide, release [Shift], click ☴ in the Animation group, scroll down, then click Loops in the Motion Paths section**

   A motion path object appears over the shapes object and identifies the direction and shape, or path, of the animation. When needed, you can move, resize, and change the direction of the motion path. Notice the numeral 2 animation tag for the shapes object indicating it is animated *after* the text object. Compare your screen to Figure D-10.

8. **Click the Move Earlier button in the Timing group, click the Slide Show tab on the Ribbon, then click the From Beginning button in the Start Slide Show group**

   The slide show begins from Slide 1. The animations make the presentation more interesting to view.

9. **When you see the black slide, press [Spacebar], then save your changes**

FIGURE D-9: Slide showing animation applied to picture

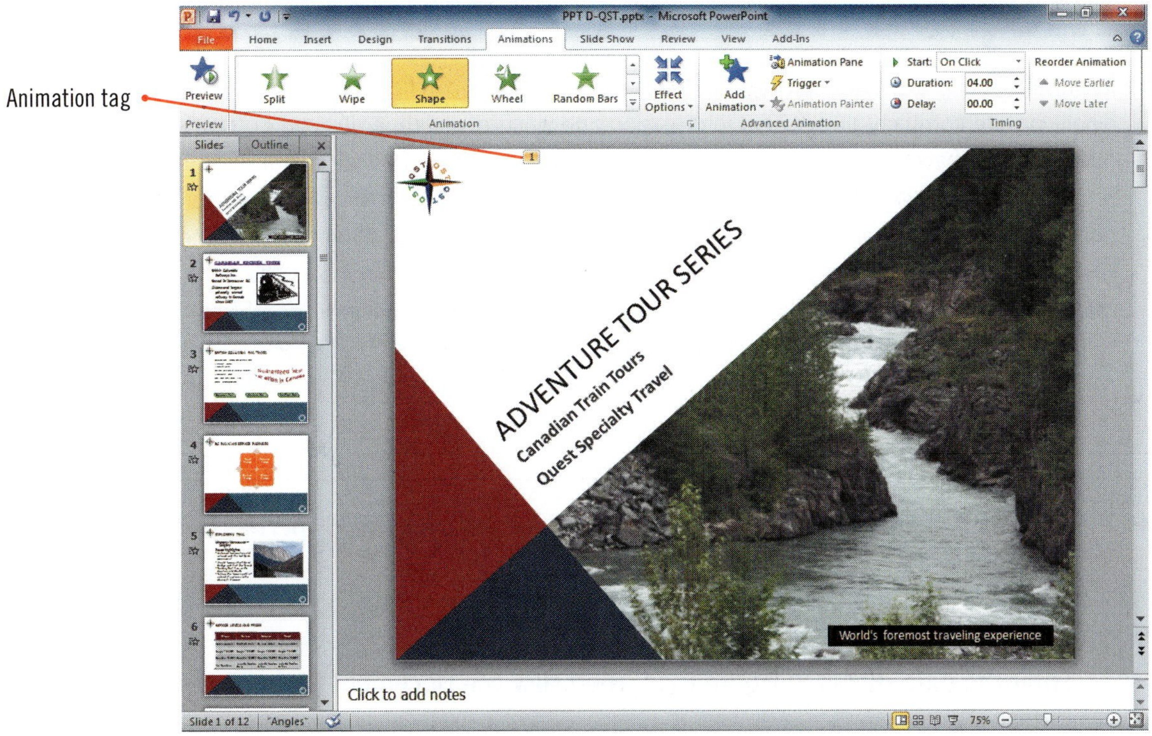

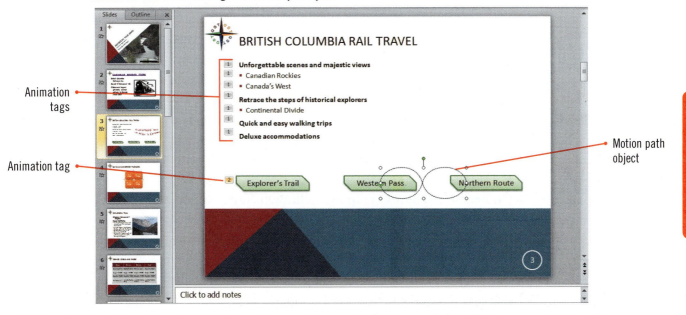

Animation tag

FIGURE D-10: Screen showing animated shapes object

Animation tags

Animation tag

Motion path object

Presentation checklist

You should always rehearse your slide show. If possible, rehearse your presentation in the room and with the computer that you will use. Use the following checklist to prepare for the slide show:

- Is PowerPoint or PowerPoint Viewer installed on the computer?
- Is your presentation file on the hard drive of the computer you will be using? Try putting a shortcut for the file on the desktop. Do you have a backup copy of your presentation file on a removable storage device, like a flash drive?
- Is the projection device working correctly? Can the slides be seen from the back of the room?

- Do you know how to control **room lighting** so the audience can see both your slides and their handouts and notes? You may want to designate someone to control the lights if the controls are not close to you.
- Will the **computer** be situated so you can advance and annotate the slides yourself? If not, designate someone to advance them for you.
- Do you have enough copies of your **handouts**? Bring extras. Decide when to hand them out, or whether you prefer to have them waiting at the audience members' seats when they enter.

Inspecting a Presentation

Reviewing your presentation can be an important step, not only to find and fix errors, but also to locate and delete private company or personal information and document properties you do not want to share with others. If you share presentations with others, especially over the Internet, it is a good idea to inspect the presentation file using the Document Inspector. The **Document Inspector** looks for hidden data and personal information that is stored in the file itself or in the document properties. Document properties, also known as **metadata**, includes specific data about the presentation, such as the author's name, subject matter, title, who saved the file last, and when the file was created. Other types of information the Document Inspector can locate and remove include presentation notes, comments, ink annotations, invisible on-slide content, off-slide content, and custom XML data. You decide to view and add some document properties, inspect your presentation file, and learn about the Mark as Final command.

STEPS

QUICK TIP
Click the Properties button, then click Advanced Properties to open the Properties dialog box to see or change more document properties.

1. **Click the File tab on the Ribbon, with Info selected, click the Properties button in the right pane, then click Show Document Panel**

   The Document Properties pane opens showing the file location and the title of the presentation. Now enter some descriptive data for this presentation file.

2. **Enter the data shown in Figure D-11, then click the Document Properties pane Close button** ☒

   This data provides detailed information about the presentation file that you can use to identify and organize your file. You can also use this information as search criteria to locate the file at a later time. You now use the Document Inspector to search for information you might want to delete in the presentation.

3. **Click the File tab on the Ribbon, with Info selected, click the Check for Issues button in the center pane, click Inspect Document, then click Yes to save the changes to the document**

   The Document Inspector dialog box opens. The Document Inspector searches the presentation file for six different types of information that you might want removed from the presentation before sharing it.

QUICK TIP
If you need to save a presentation to run in an earlier version of PowerPoint, check for unsupported features using the Check Compatibility feature.

4. **Make sure all of the check boxes are selected, then click Inspect**

   The presentation file is reviewed, and the results are shown in Figure D-12. The Document Inspector found items having to do with document properties, which you just entered, and presentation notes, which are on Slides 11 and 12. You decide to leave the document properties alone but delete the notes for all of the slides.

5. **Click the Remove All button in the Presentation Notes section, then click Close**

   All notes are removed from the Notes pane for the slides in the presentation.

6. **Click the Protect Presentation button, click Mark as Final, then click OK in the alert box**

   A message box opens. Be sure to read the message to understand what happens to the file and how to recognize a marked-as-final presentation. You decide to complete this procedure.

QUICK TIP
Presentations marked as final in PowerPoint 2010 are not read-only if they are opened in earlier versions of PowerPoint.

7. **Click OK, click the Home tab on the Ribbon, click the Slide 1 thumbnail in the Slides tab, then click anywhere in the title text object**

   Notice in Figure D-13 that the Ribbon is no longer displayed and an information alert box notes that the presentation is marked as final, making it a read-only file. A **read-only** file is one that can't be edited or modified in any way. Anyone who has received a read-only presentation can only edit the presentation by changing its marked-as-final status. You still want to work on the presentation, so you remove the marked-as-final status.

8. **Click the Edit Anyway button in the information alert box, then save your changes**

   The Ribbon and all commands are active again, and the file can now be modified.

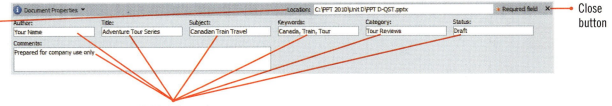

Your file location will be different

Add this information

Close button

FIGURE D-12: Document Inspector dialog box

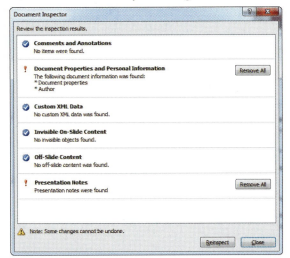

FIGURE D-13: Marked as final presentation

Identifies the file as read-only

Information alert box

Digitally sign a presentation

What is a digital signature, and why would you want to use one in PowerPoint? A **digital signature** is similar to a hand-written signature in that it authenticates your document; however, a digital signature, unlike a hand-written signature, is created using computer cryptography and is not visible within the presentation itself. There are three primary reasons you would add a digital signature to a presentation: one, to authenticate the signer of the document; two, to assure that the content of the presentation has not been changed since it was signed; and three, to assure the origin of the signed document. To add a digital signature, click the File tab on the Ribbon, click the Protect Presentation button, click Add a Digital Signature, then follow the dialog boxes.

Evaluating a Presentation

A well-designed and organized presentation requires thought and preparation. An effective presentation is focused and visually appealing—easy for the speaker to present and simple for the audience to understand. Visual elements can strongly influence the audience's attention and can influence the success of your presentation. See Table D-3 for general information on the impact a visual presentation has on an audience. 🎨 You know your boss and other colleagues will critique your presentation, so you take the time to evaluate your presentation's organization and effectiveness.

STEPS

1. Click the Reading View button 📖 on the status bar, then press [Spacebar] when the slide show finishes

QUICK TIP
You can also move, delete, collapse, and expand a section in the Slides tab or in Slide Sorter view.

2. Click the Slide 5 thumbnail in the Slides tab, click the Section button in the Slides group, then click Add Section

   Two new sections appear in the Slides tab, the section you created, called the Untitled Section and a section for all the slides before the new section, called the Default Section. Sections help you organize your slides into logical groups.

3. Right-click Untitled Section in the Slides tab, click Rename Section, type Tour Packages, then click Rename

4. Click the Slide Sorter view button 🔲 on the status bar, save your work, then compare your screen to Figure D-14

5. Double-click Slide 1, add your name to the notes and handouts footer, evaluate your presentation according to the guidelines below, submit your presentation to your instructor, then close the presentation

   Figure D-15 shows a poorly designed slide. Contrast this slide with guidelines below and your presentation.

DETAILS

When evaluating a presentation, it is important to:

- **Keep your message focused and your text concise**

  Don't put every point you plan to say on your slides. Keep the audience anticipating explanations to the key points in the presentation. Limit each slide to six words per line and six lines per slide. Use bulleted lists to help prioritize your points visually. Your presentation text should only provide highlights of your message. Supplement the information on your slides with further explanation and details during your presentation.

- **Keep the design simple, easy to read, and appropriate for the content**

  A design theme makes the presentation consistent. If you design your own layout, keep it simple and use design elements sparingly. Use similar design elements consistently throughout the presentation; otherwise, your audience may get confused.

- **Choose attractive colors that make the slide easy to read**

  Use contrasting colors for slide background and text to make the text readable. If you are giving an on-screen presentation, you can use almost any combination of colors that look good together.

- **Choose fonts and styles that are easy to read and emphasize important text**

  As a general rule, use no more than two fonts in a presentation and vary the font size, using nothing smaller than 24 points. Use bold and italic attributes selectively.

- **Use visuals to help communicate the message of your presentation**

  Commonly used visuals include clip art, photographs, charts, worksheets, tables, and videos. Whenever possible, replace text with a visual, but be careful not to overcrowd your slides. White space on your slides is okay!

FIGURE D-14: The final presentation in Slide Sorter view

New default section

New renamed section

FIGURE D-15: A poorly designed slide

Too many fonts and font styles used

Too many words used

Shape serves no purpose and does not fit theme

Theme does not fit content

Duplicate clip art not necessary

Too many font colors

Too much text on the slide

Font is hard to read and is lost on the slide

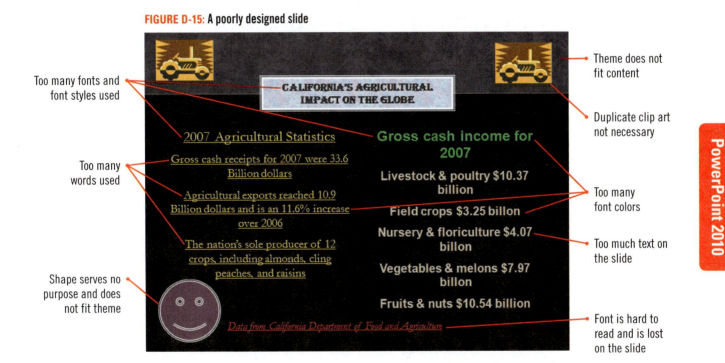

TABLE D-3: Audience impact from a visual presentation

impact	description
Visual reception	75% of all environmental stimuli is received through visual reception
Learning	55% of what an audience learns comes directly from visual messages
Retention	Combining visual messages with verbal messages can increase memory retention by as much as 50%
Presentation goals	You are twice as likely (67%) to achieve your communication objectives using a visual presentation
Meeting length	You are likely to decrease the average meeting length by 26.8% when you use a visual presentation

Source: Presenters Online, www.presentersonline.com

Creating a Template

When planning the design of your presentation, keep in mind that you are not limited to using the standard themes PowerPoint provides or the ones you find on the Web. You can also create a presentation using a template. A **template** is a type of presentation file that contains custom design elements on the slide master, background, slide layouts, and a theme, and can include graphics and content. You can create a new template from a blank presentation, or you can modify an existing PowerPoint presentation and save it as a template. If you modify an existing presentation, you can modify or delete any color, graphic, or font as necessary. When you save a presentation as a template file the .potx extension is added to the filename. You can then use your template presentation as the basis for new presentations. You are finished working on your presentation for now. You want to create a template using the design theme of this presentation so others can use it.

1. **Click the File tab on the Ribbon, click New, make sure Blank presentation is selected in the Available Templates and Themes section, then click Create**

   A new presentation appears. Now save this presentation as a template.

2. **Click the File tab on the Ribbon, click Save As, click the Save as type list arrow, then click PowerPoint Template (*.potx)**

   Because this is a template, PowerPoint automatically opens the Templates folder on your hard drive.

   QUICK TIP

   Presentations saved to the Templates folder appear in the Recent templates folder. To locate this folder, click the File tab on the Ribbon, click New, then click Recent templates.

3. **Locate the drive and folder where you store your Data Files, click to select the default filename Presentation 1 in the File name text box, type PPT D-QST Template as shown in Figure D-16, then click Save**

   The presentation is saved as a PowerPoint template to the drive and folder where you store your Data Files, and the new template presentation appears in the PowerPoint window.

4. **Click the Design tab on the Ribbon, click the More button ⏷ in the Themes group, then click Browse for Themes**

   The Choose Theme or Themed Document dialog box opens.

5. **Locate the drive and folder where you store your Data Files, click PPT D-QST, then click Apply**

   The design theme, including slide transitions and slide timings, from the presentation PPT D-QST is applied to the PPT D-QST Template presentation. All slide master elements, including slide layouts, colors, shapes, fonts, and background elements from the PPT D-QST presentation are applied over the existing design theme of the PPT D-QST Template presentation.

   QUICK TIP

   To quickly replace a word you have typed with a common synonym, right-click the word, then point to Synonyms on the shortcut menu.

6. **Click the title text placeholder, type QST Template, click the subtitle placeholder, type Standard Company Use Template – Your Name, then save your changes**

   You don't need to keep the slide transitions and slide timings that were applied from the PPT D-QST presentation.

7. **Click the Transitions tab on the Ribbon, click the More button ⏷ in the Transition to This Slide group, click None, click the After check box in the Timing group, then click the Apply to All button in the Timing group**

   The slide transitions and slide timing are removed from the presentation.

8. **Click the View tab, click the Slide Sorter button in the Presentation Views group, then drag the Zoom Slider all the way to the right**

   Figure D-17 shows the final template presentation in Slide Sorter view.

9. **Double-click Slide 1, save your work, submit your presentation to your instructor, close the presentation, then exit PowerPoint**

FIGURE D-16: Save As dialog box

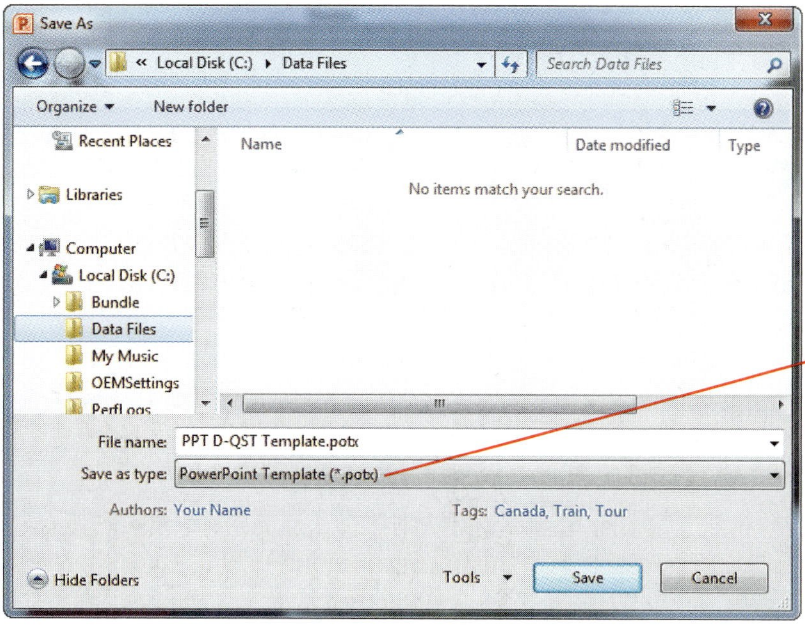

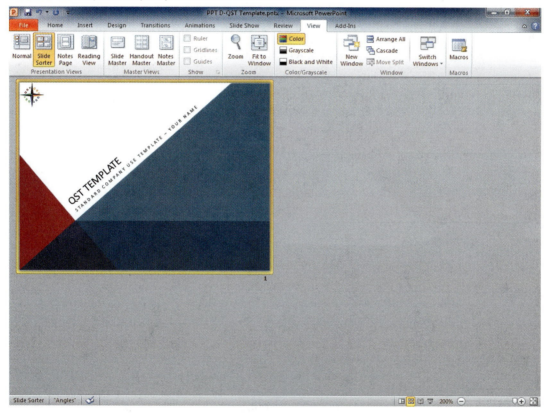

PowerPoint template file type

FIGURE D-17: Completed template presentation in Slide Sorter view

Using Paste Special

Paste Special is used to paste text or objects into PowerPoint using a specific file format. For example, you may want to paste some text as a picture or as plain text without formatting. Copy the text, then in PowerPoint click the Paste list arrow, click Paste Special, then select the appropriate file format option. You can also link an object or selected information from another program to PowerPoint using the Paste Special command. This technique is useful when you want to link part of an Excel worksheet or a chart from a workbook that contains both a worksheet and a chart. To link just the chart, open the Microsoft Excel worksheet, then copy the chart. Leaving Excel and the source file open, click the Paste list arrow, click Paste Special, click the Paste link option button, then click OK.

Practice

Concepts Review

For current SAM information, including versions and content details, visit SAM Central (http://www.cengage.com/samcentral). If you have a SAM user profile, you may have access to hands-on instruction, practice, and assessment of the skills covered in this unit. Since various versions of SAM are supported throughout the life of this text, check with your instructor for the correct instructions and URL/Web site for accessing assignments.

Label each element of the PowerPoint window shown in Figure D-18.

FIGURE D-18

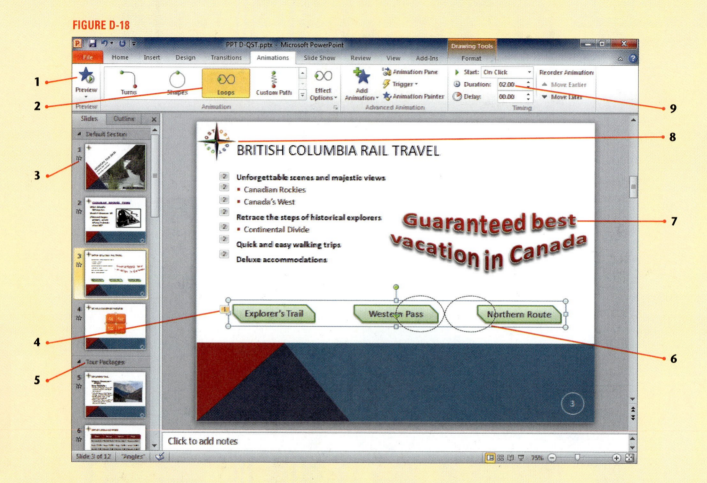

Match each term with the statement that best describes it.

10. Masters   **a.** Identifies the order in which objects are animated

11. Annotate   **b.** The area behind text and graphics

12. Metadata   **c.** Includes document properties such as the author's name

13. Animation tag   **d.** To draw on a slide during a slide show

14. Transitions   **e.** Slides that store theme and placeholder information

15. Background   **f.** Visual effects that determine how a slide moves in and out of view during a slide show

Select the best answer from the list of choices.

16. **The effect that determines how a slide moves in and out of view during a slide show is called a(n):**
    a. Transition.
    b. Timing.
    c. Theme.
    d. Animation.

17. **An object placed on the slide master defines which of the following items?**
    a. Background graphic
    b. Logo
    c. Shape
    d. Master placeholder

18. **Which of the following statements about masters is *not* true?**
    a. Each slide layout in the presentation has a corresponding slide layout in Slide Master view.
    b. The design theme is placed on the slide master.
    c. Masters store information.
    d. Changes made to the slide master are reflected in the handout and notes masters as well.

19. **Which PowerPoint file *can't* be edited or modified?**
    a. Inspected file
    b. File saved in another file format
    c. Read-only file
    d. Template file

20. **The effect that controls how an object appears on the screen during a slide show is called a(n):**
    a. Transition.
    b. Animation.
    c. Path.
    d. Template.

21. **The Document Inspector looks for _____ and personal information that is stored in the presentation file.**
    a. themes
    b. hidden data
    c. animation tags
    d. video settings

22. **According to the book, which standard should you follow to evaluate a presentation?**
    a. Replace visuals with text as often as possible.
    b. Slides should include most of the information you wish to present.
    c. Use many different design elements to keep your audience from getting bored.
    d. The message should be outlined in a concise way.

Skills Review

1. **Modify masters.**
   a. Open the presentation PPT D-3.pptx from the drive and folder where you store your Data Files, then save the presentation as **PPT D-New Product**.
   b. Open Slide Master view using the View tab, then click the Origin Slide Master thumbnail.
   c. Insert the picture PPT D-4.jpg, then resize the picture so it is 0.8" wide.
   d. Drag the picture to the upper-right corner of the slide within the design frame of the slide, then deselect the picture.
   e. Preserve the Origin master, switch to Normal view, then save your changes.

2. **Customize the background and theme.**
   a. Switch to Slide 3, click the Design tab, then open the background styles gallery.
   b. Change the background style to Style 5.
   c. Open the Format Background dialog box.
   d. Set the Transparency to 25%, apply the background to all of the slides, then close the dialog box.
   e. Click the Colors button, then click Office. Click the Fonts button, then click Office Classic 2.
   f. Save your changes.

3. **Use slide show commands.**
   a. Begin the slide show on Slide 1, then proceed to Slide 4.
   b. Use the Pen to circle the words **Early Adopters**, **Mass Adopters**, and **Late Adopters**.
   c. Move to Slide 5, then use the Highlighter to highlight the words **Pricing**, **Look**, and **Fulfillment issues**.

    d. Right-click the slide and go to Slide 1, move to Slide 4, then erase all ink on the slide.

    e. Move to Slide 5, erase the ink on the slide, then change the pointer back to ▷.

    f. Press [Home], advance through the slide show, don't save any ink annotations, then save your work.

4. Set slide transitions and timings.

    a. Go to Slide Sorter view, click the Slide 1 thumbnail, then apply the Vortex transition to the slide.

    b. Change the effect option to From Bottom, change the duration speed to 3.00, then apply to all the slides.

    c. Change the slide timing to 5 seconds, then apply to all of the slides.

    d. Switch to Normal view, view the slide show, then save your work.

5. Animate objects.

    a. Go to Slide 3, click the Animations tab, then select the E shape on the slide.

    b. Apply the Swivel effect to the object, click the Price arrow, apply the Float In effect, then preview the animations.

    c. On Slide 4 apply the Spin effect (Emphasis section) to the title text object.

    d. Select the six objects in the graphic, click the More button in the Animation group, click More Entrance Effects, then apply an animation of your choice from the Exciting group to the six selected objects in the graphic.

    e. Apply animation effects to objects on at least two more slides in the presentation.

    f. Edit the animations effects as needed, then save your changes.

6. Inspect a presentation.

    a. Open the Document Properties pane, type **Internet Product** in the Subject text box, then type **Review** in the Status text box.

    b. Close the Document Properties pane, then open the Document Inspector dialog box.

    c. Make sure the Off-Slide Content check box is selected, then inspect the presentation.

    d. Delete the off-slide content and the presentation notes, then close the dialog box. Save your changes.

7. Evaluate a presentation.

    a. Go to Slide 1, then run a slide show.

    b. Evaluate the presentation using the points described in the lesson as criteria, then submit a written evaluation to your instructor.

    c. Move Slide 6 below Slide 8.

    d. Check the spelling of the presentation, add the slide number and your name to the slide footer on all the slides, then save your changes.

    e. Switch to Slide Sorter view, then compare your presentation to Figure D-19.

    f. Submit your presentation to your instructor, then close the presentation.

FIGURE D-19

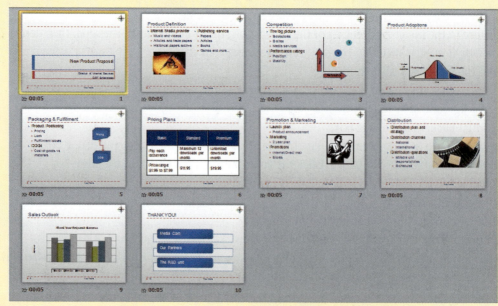

8. **Create a template.**

   a. Create a new presentation, then save it as a PowerPoint template with the name **PPT D-Template** to the drive and folder where your Data Files are stored.

   b. Click the More button in the Themes group, browse for themes, locate the drive and folder where you store your Data files, click PPT D-New Product, then click Apply.

   c. Type **QST Template** in the title placeholder, then type your name in the subtitle placeholder.

   d. Delete the slide transitions and animations, remove the slide timing, then select the On Mouse Click option in the Timing group.

   e. Save your work, then submit your presentation to your instructor.

   f. Close the presentation, then exit PowerPoint.

Independent Challenge 1

You are a travel consultant for Island Travel Services, located in Tampa, Florida. You have been working on a sales presentation that is going to be accessed by customers on the company Web site. You need to finish up what you have been working on by adding transitions, timings, and animation effects to the sales presentation.

If you have a SAM 2010 user profile, an autogradable SAM version of this assignment may be available at http://www.cengage.com/sam2010. Check with your instructor to confirm that this assignment is available in SAM. To use the SAM version of this assignment, log into the SAM 2010 Web site and download the instruction and start files.

   a. Open the file PPT D-5.pptx from the drive and folder where you store your Data Files, and save the presentation as **PPT D-Island**.

   b. Add the slide number and your name as the footer on all slides, except the title slide.

   c. Apply the Float In animation to the title text on each slide.

   d. Apply the Wipe animation to the bulleted text objects on each slide.

   e. Apply the Shape animation to the table on Slide 8, then change the effect option to Box.

   f. Apply the Shred slide transition, apply a 7-second slide timing, then apply to all of the slides.

   g. Check the spelling of the presentation, then save your changes.

   h. View the slide show, and evaluate your presentation. Make changes if necessary.

   i. Submit your presentation to your instructor, close the presentation, then exit PowerPoint.

Independent Challenge 2

You are a development engineer at Extreme Sports, Inc., an international sports product design company located in Fargo, North Dakota. Extreme Sports designs and manufactures items such as bike helmets, bike racks, and kayak paddles, and markets these items primarily to countries in North America and Western Europe. You need to finish the work on a quarterly presentation that outlines the progress of the company's newest technologies by adding animations, customizing the background, and using the Document Inspector.

   a. Open the file PPT D-6.pptx from the drive and folder where you store your Data Files, and save the presentation as **PPT D-Extreme**.

   b. Apply an appropriate design theme, then apply a new slide background style. Make sure the new background style is appropriate for the design theme you have chosen.

   c. Apply the Ripple slide transition to all slides, then animate the following objects: the text on Slide 2, the clip art object on Slide 3, the table on Slide 4, and the clip art on Slide 6. View the slide show to evaluate the effects you added and make adjustments as necessary.

   d. Run the Document Inspector with all options selected, identify what items the Document Inspector finds, close the Document Inspector dialog box, then review the slides to find the items.

Independent Challenge 2 (continued)

e. Add a slide at the end of the presentation that identifies the items the Document Inspector found.

f. Run the Document Inspector again, and remove all items except the document properties.

Advanced Challenge Exercise

- Click the Rehearse Timings button on the Slide Sorter toolbar.
- Set slide timings for each slide in the presentation.
- Save new slide timings.

g. Add your name as a footer to all slides, run the spell checker, save your work, then run a slide show to evaluate your presentation.

h. Submit your presentation to your instructor, then close the presentation and exit PowerPoint.

Independent Challenge 3

You work for Young & Associates, a full-service investment and pension firm. Your boss wants you to create a presentation on small business pension plan options to be published on the company Web site. You have completed adding the information to the presentation, now you need to add a design theme, format some information, add some animation effects, and add slide timings.

a. Open the file PPT D-7.pptx from the drive and folder where you store your Data Files, and save the presentation as **PPT D-IRAPlans**.

b. Apply an appropriate design theme.

c. Apply animation effects to the following objects: the shapes on Slide 3 and the text and clip art on Slide 5. View the slide show to evaluate the effects you added, and make adjustments as necessary.

d. Convert the text on Slide 4 to a Basic Radial SmartArt graphic (Found in the Cycle category).

e. Apply the Intense Effect style to the SmartArt graphic, then change the colors of the graphic to Colorful Range – Accent Colors 2 to 3.

f. Switch to Slide 3, align the Sector and Quality arrow shapes to one another, then align the Allocation and Maturity arrow shapes to one another.

g. Adjust the aligned arrow shapes so they are centered on the Buy/Sell oval shape, then apply a 15-second timing to Slides 3–7 and a 5-second timing to Slides 1 and 2.

h. Add a section between Slide 5 and Slide 6, then rename the section **Plans**.

i. Rename the Default section in the Slides tab to **Intro**.

Advanced Challenge Exercise

- Open Slide Master view, select the last slide layout, then click the Insert Layout button.
- Click the Insert Placeholder list arrow, click Table, then drag a placeholder in the blank area of the Slide Master layout. (*Hint*: Draw the table placeholder so it takes up most of the blank space in the layout.)
- Return to Normal view, apply the new Custom Layout to Slides 6 and 7. Adjust the placeholder in Slide Master view if necessary.

j. Add your name as a footer to the slides, run the spell checker, save your work, then run a slide show to evaluate your presentation.

k. Submit your presentation to your instructor, then close the presentation and exit PowerPoint.

Real Life Independent Challenge

You work for the operations supervisor at the Tennessee State University student union. Create a presentation that you can eventually publish to the college Web site that describes all of the services offered at the student union.

a. Plan and create the slide presentation that describes the services and events offered at the student union. To help create content, use the student union at your school or use the Internet to locate information on college student unions. The presentation should contain at least six slides.

b. Use an appropriate design theme.

c. Add clip art and photographs available in the Clip Organizer, then style and customize at least one photo.

d. Save the presentation as **PPT D-TSU** to the drive and folder where you store your Data Files. View the slide show, and evaluate the contents of your presentation. Make any necessary adjustments.

e. Add slide transitions, animation effects, and timings to the presentation. View the slide show again to evaluate the effects you added.

f. Add your name as a footer to the slides. Spell check the presentation, save, inspect, then submit your presentation to your instructor. An example of a finished presentation is shown in Figure D-20.

g. Create a template from this presentation using a new presentation, then save the presentation as **PPT D-TSU Template** to the drive and folder where you store your Data Files.

h. Type **TSU Template** in the title placeholder, type your name in the subtitle placeholder, delete transitions and animations, submit your presentation to your instructor, close the template presentation, then exit PowerPoint.

FIGURE D-20

Visual Workshop

Create a new PowerPoint template (.potx) with the filename **PPT D-School Template** and save it to the drive and folder where you store your Data Files. Change the presentation to look like Figures D-21 and D-22. Figure D-22 shows a slide with a custom slide layout that you need to create. Submit your presentation to your instructor.

FIGURE D-21

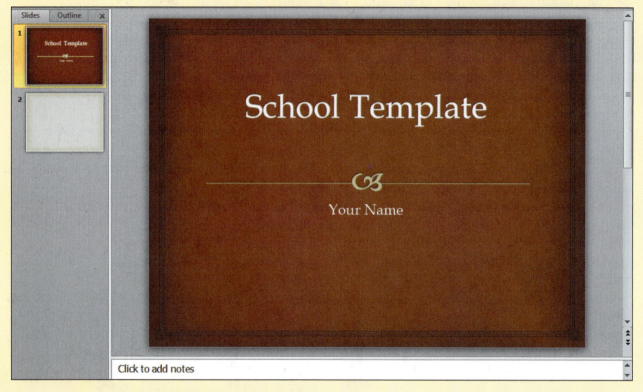

FIGURE D-22

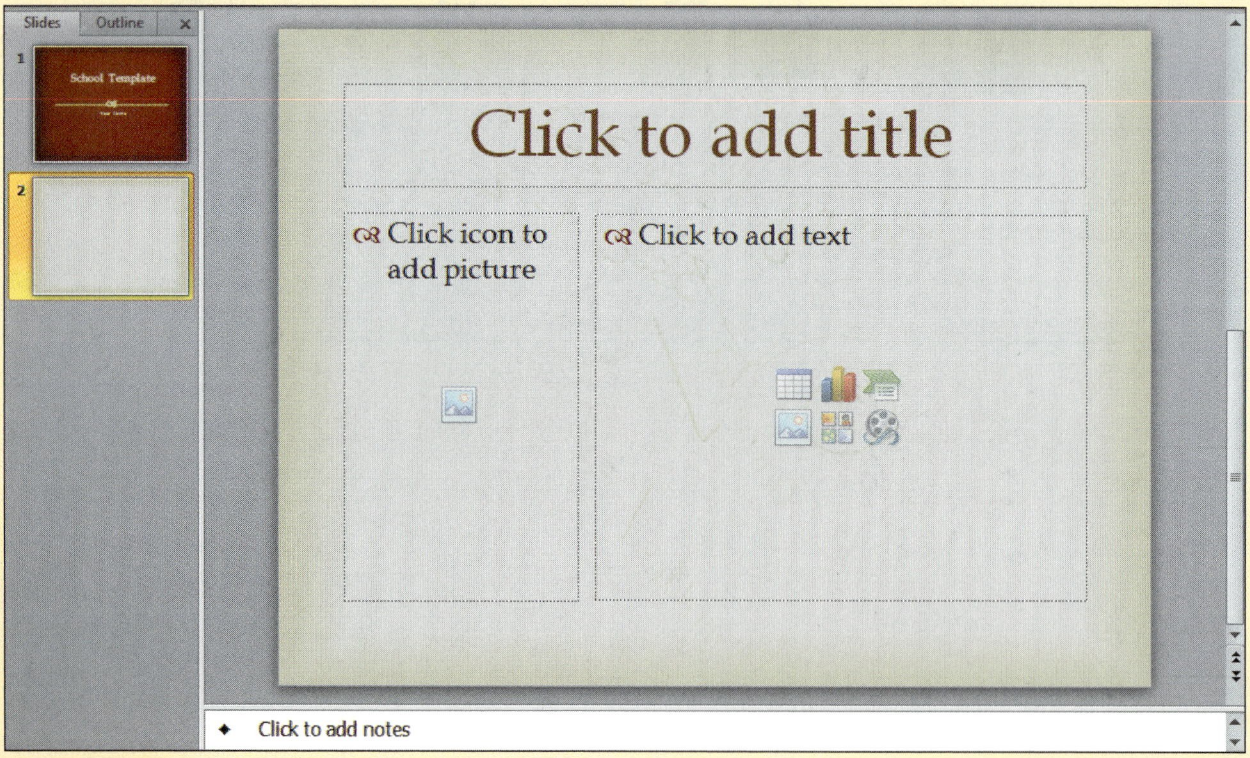

Working with Windows Live and Office Web Apps

If the computer you are using has an active Internet connection, you can go to the Microsoft Windows Live Web site and access a wide variety of services and Web applications. For example, you can check your e-mail through Windows Live, network with your friends and coworkers, and use SkyDrive to store and share files. From SkyDrive, you can also use Office Web Apps to create and edit Word, PowerPoint, Excel, and OneNote files, even when you are using a computer that does not have Office 2010 installed. You work in the Vancouver branch of Quest Specialty Travel. Your supervisor, Mary Lou Jacobs, asks you to explore Windows Live and learn how she can use SkyDrive and Office Web Apps to work with her files online.

(*Note*: SkyDrive and Office Web Apps are dynamic Web pages, and might change over time, including the way they are organized and how commands are performed. The steps and figures in this appendix were accurate at the time this book was published.)

OBJECTIVES

Explore how to work online from Windows Live

Obtain a Windows Live ID and sign in to Windows Live

Upload files to Windows Live

Work with the PowerPoint Web App

Create folders and organize files on SkyDrive

Add people to your network and share files

Work with the Excel Web App

Exploring How to Work Online from Windows Live

You can use your Web browser to upload your files to Windows Live from any computer connected to the Internet. You can work on the files right in your Web browser using Office Web Apps and share your files with people in your Windows Live network. You review the concepts and services related to working online from Windows Live.

DETAILS

- ### What is Windows Live?

  Windows Live is a collection of services and Web applications that you can use to help you be more productive both personally and professionally. For example, you can use Windows Live to send and receive e-mail, to chat with friends via instant messaging, to share photos, to create a blog, and to store and edit files using SkyDrive. Table WEB-1 describes the services available on Windows Live. Windows Live is a free service that you sign up for. When you sign up, you receive a Windows Live ID, which you use to sign in to Windows Live. When you work with files on Windows Live, you are cloud computing.

- ### What is Cloud Computing?

  The term **cloud computing** refers to the process of working with files online in a Web browser. When you save files to SkyDrive on Windows Live, you are saving your files to an online location. SkyDrive is like having a personal hard drive in the cloud.

- ### What is SkyDrive?

  SkyDrive is an online storage and file sharing service. With a Windows Live account, you receive access to your own SkyDrive, which is your personal storage area on the Internet. On your SkyDrive, you are given space to store up to 25 GB of data online. Each file can be a maximum size of 50 MB. You can also use SkyDrive to access Office Web Apps, which you use to create and edit files created in Word, OneNote, PowerPoint, and Excel online in your Web browser.

- ### Why use Windows Live and SkyDrive?

  On Windows Live, you use SkyDrive to access additional storage for your files. You don't have to worry about backing up your files to a memory stick or other storage device that could be lost or damaged. Another advantage of storing your files on SkyDrive is that you can access your files from any computer that has an active Internet connection. Figure WEB-1 shows the SkyDrive Web page that appears when accessed from a Windows Live account. From SkyDrive, you can also access Office Web Apps.

- ### What are Office Web Apps?

  Office Web Apps are versions of Microsoft Word, Excel, PowerPoint, and OneNote that you can access online from your SkyDrive. An Office Web App does not include all of the features and functions included with the full Office version of its associated application. However, you can use the Office Web App from any computer that is connected to the Internet, even if Microsoft Office 2010 is not installed on that computer.

- ### How do SkyDrive and Office Web Apps work together?

  You can create a file in Office 2010 using Word, Excel, PowerPoint, or OneNote and then upload the file to your SkyDrive. You can then open the Office file saved to SkyDrive and edit it using your Web browser and the corresponding Office Web App. Figure WEB-2 shows a PowerPoint presentation open in the PowerPoint Web App. You can also use an Office Web App to create a new file, which is saved automatically to SkyDrive while you work. In addition, you can download a file created with an Office Web App and continue to work with the file in the full version of the corresponding Office application: Word, Excel, PowerPoint, or OneNote. Finally, you can create a SkyDrive network that consists of the people you want to be able to view your folders and files on your SkyDrive. You can give people permission to view and edit your files using any computer with an active Internet connection and a Web browser.

FIGURE WEB-1: SkyDrive on Windows Live

Browser window

SkyDrive - Windows Live tab

By default, one folder is available on SkyDrive; you can create additional folders

The name of the person who signed into Windows Live and SkyDrive appears here

Monitors the amount of space still available on your SkyDrive

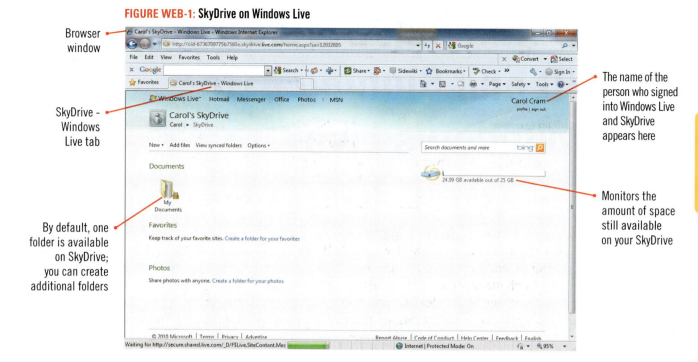

FIGURE WEB-2: PowerPoint presentation open in the PowerPoint Web App

Browser window

Ribbon available in PowerPoint Web App

The presentation in PowerPoint Web App maintains the same look and feel as the same presentation in the desktop version of PowerPoint

Name of PowerPoint presentation open in PowerPoint Web App

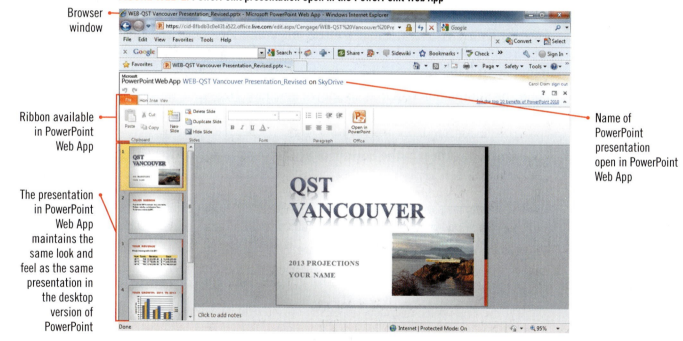

TABLE WEB-1: Services available via Windows Live

service	description
E-mail	Send and receive e-mail using a Hotmail account
Instant Messaging	Use Messenger to chat with friends, share photos, and play games
SkyDrive	Store files, work on files using Office Web Apps, and share files with people in your network
Photos	Upload and share photos with friends
People	Develop a network of friends and coworkers, then use the network to distribute information and stay in touch
Downloads	Access a variety of free programs available for download to a PC
Mobile Device	Access applications for a mobile device: text messaging, using Hotmail, networking, and sharing photos

Obtaining a Windows Live ID and Signing In to Windows Live

To work with your files online using SkyDrive and Office Web Apps, you need a Windows Live ID. You obtain a Windows Live ID by going to the Windows Live Web site and creating a new account. Once you have a Windows Live ID, you can access SkyDrive and then use it to store your files, create new files, and share your files with friends and coworkers. Mary Lou Jacobs, your supervisor at QST Vancouver, asks you to obtain a Windows Live ID so that you can work on documents with your coworkers. You go to the Windows Live Web site, create a Windows Live ID, and then sign in to your SkyDrive.

STEPS

QUICK TIP

If you already have a Windows Live ID, go to the next lesson and sign in as directed using your account.

1. **Open your Web browser, type home.live.com in the Address bar, then press [Enter]**

   The Windows Live home page opens. From this page, you can create a Windows Live account and receive your Windows Live ID.

2. **Click the Sign up button** *(Note: You may see a Sign up link instead of a button)*

   The Create your Windows Live ID page opens.

3. **Click the Or use your own e-mail address link under the Check availability button or if you are already using Hotmail, Messenger, or Xbox LIVE, click the Sign in now link in the Information statement near the top of the page**

4. **Enter the information required, as shown in Figure WEB-3**

   If you wish, you can sign up for a Windows Live e-mail address such as yourname@live.com so that you can also access the Windows Live e-mail services.

TROUBLE

The code can be difficult to read. If you receive an error message, enter the new code that appears.

5. **Enter the code shown at the bottom of your screen, then click the I accept button**

   The Windows Live home page opens. The name you entered when you signed up for your Windows Live ID appears in the top right corner of the window to indicate that you are signed in to Windows Live. From the Windows Live home page, you can access all the services and applications offered by Windows Live. See the Verifying your Windows Live ID box for information on finalizing your account set up.

6. **Point to Windows Live, as shown in Figure WEB-4**

   A list of options appears. SkyDrive is one of the options you can access directly from Windows Live.

TROUBLE

Click I accept if you are asked to review and accept the Windows Live Service Agreement and Privacy Statement.

7. **Click SkyDrive**

   The SkyDrive page opens. Your name appears in the top right corner, and the amount of space available is shown on the right side of the SkyDrive page. The amount of space available is monitored, as indicated by the gauge that fills with color as space is used. Using SkyDrive, you can add files to the existing folder and you can create new folders.

8. **Click sign out in the top right corner under your name, then exit the Web browser**

   You are signed out of your Windows Live account. You can sign in again directly from the Windows Live page in your browser or from within a file created with PowerPoint, Excel, Word, or OneNote.

FIGURE WEB-3: Creating a Windows Live ID

Click to sign in using a Hotmail, Messenger, or Xbox Live account

Once your registration is complete, you will be asked to verify your ID

A different code will appear on your screen

Type your e-mail address

You can choose to get a Windows Live e-mail address

Enter the information required

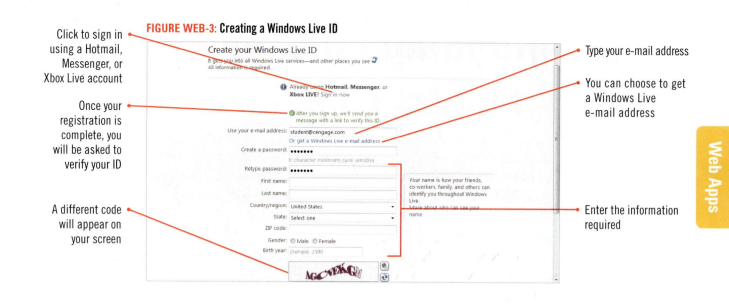

FIGURE WEB-4: Selecting SkyDrive

SkyDrive in the list of Windows Live options

Information about your Windows Live network

Your name appears here

Click to quickly add people to your network

An advertisement appropriate for your location appears here

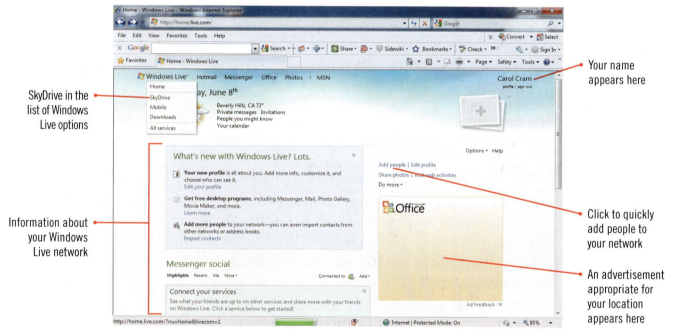

Verifying your Windows Live ID

As soon as you accept the Windows Live terms, an e-mail is sent to the e-mail address you supplied when you created your Windows Live ID. Open your e-mail program, and then open the e-mail from Microsoft with the Subject line: Confirm your e-mail address for Windows Live. Follow the simple, step-by-step instructions in the e-mail to confirm your Windows Live ID. When the confirmation is complete, you will be asked to sign in to Windows Live, using your e-mail address and password. Once signed in, you will see your Windows Live Account page.

Uploading Files to Windows Live

Once you have created your Windows Live ID, you can sign in to Windows Live directly from Word, PowerPoint, Excel, or OneNote and start saving and uploading files. You upload files to your SkyDrive so you can share the files with other people, access the files from another computer, or use SkyDrive's additional storage. ▓▓▓▓ You open a PowerPoint presentation, access your Windows Live account from Backstage view, and save a file to SkyDrive on Windows Live. You also create a new folder called Cengage directly from Backstage view and add a file to it.

STEPS

1. **Start PowerPoint, open the file WEB-1.pptx from the drive and folder where you store your Data Files, then save the file as WEB-QST Vancouver Presentation**

2. **Click the File tab, then click Save & Send**

   The Save & Send options available in PowerPoint are listed in Backstage view, as shown in Figure WEB-5.

3. **Click Save to Web**

QUICK TIP
Skip this step if the computer you are using signs you in automatically.

4. **Click Sign In, type your e-mail address, press [Tab], type your password, then click OK**

   The My Documents folder on your SkyDrive appears in the Save to Windows Live SkyDrive information area.

5. **Click Save As, wait a few seconds for the Save As dialog box to appear, then click Save**

   The file is saved to the My Documents folder on the SkyDrive that is associated with your Windows Live account. You can also create a new folder and upload files directly to SkyDrive from your hard drive.

6. **Click the File tab, click Save & Send, click Save to Web, then sign in if the My Documents folder does not automatically appear in Backstage view**

7. **Click the New Folder button in the Save to Windows Live SkyDrive pane, then sign in to Windows Live if directed**

8. **Type Cengage as the folder name, click Next, then click Add files**

9. **Click select documents from your computer, then navigate to the location on your computer where you saved the file WEB-QST Vancouver Presentation in Step 1**

10. **Click WEB-QST Vancouver Presentation.pptx to select it, then click Open**

    You can continue to add more files; however, you have no more files to upload at this time.

11. **Click Continue**

    In a few moments, the PowerPoint presentation is uploaded to your SkyDrive, as shown in Figure WEB-6. You can simply store the file on SkyDrive or you can choose to work on the presentation using the PowerPoint Web App.

12. **Click the PowerPoint icon 📄 on your taskbar to return to PowerPoint, then close the presentation and exit PowerPoint**

FIGURE WEB-5: Save & Send options in Backstage view

PowerPoint file

Save & Send area in Backstage view

Save to Web option

FIGURE WEB-6: File uploaded to the Cengage folder on Windows Live

Browser window

Path to file

Current folder menu bar

Uploaded file

Working with the PowerPoint Web App

Once you have uploaded a file to SkyDrive on Windows Live, you can work on it using its corresponding Office Web App. **Office Web Apps** provide you with the tools you need to view documents online and to edit them right in your browser. You do not need to have Office programs installed on the computer you use to access SkyDrive and Office Web Apps. From SkyDrive, you can also open the document directly in the full Office application (for example, PowerPoint) if the application is installed on the computer you are using. You use the PowerPoint Web App to make some edits to the PowerPoint presentation. You then open the presentation in PowerPoint and use the full version to make additional edits.

STEPS

TROUBLE

Click the browser button on the task-bar, then click the Windows Live SkyDrive window to make it the active window.

1. **Click the WEB-QST Vancouver Presentation file in the Cengage folder on SkyDrive**

   The presentation opens in your browser window. A menu is available, which includes the options you have for working with the file.

2. **Click Edit in Browser, then if a message appears related to installing the Sign-in Assistant, click the Close button ☒ to the far right of the message**

   In a few moments, the PowerPoint presentation opens in the PowerPoint Web App, as shown in Figure WEB-7. Table WEB-2 lists the commands you can perform using the PowerPoint Web App.

QUICK TIP

The changes you make to the presen-tation are saved automatically on SkyDrive.

3. **Enter your name where indicated on Slide 1, click Slide 3 (New Tours) in the Slides pane, then click Delete Slide in the Slides group**

   The slide is removed from the presentation. You decide to open the file in the full version of PowerPoint on your computer so you can apply WordArt to the slide title. You work with the file in the full version of PowerPoint when you want to use functions, such as WordArt, that are not available on the PowerPoint Web App.

4. **Click Open in PowerPoint in the Office group, click OK in response to the message, then click Allow if requested**

   In a few moments, the revised version of the PowerPoint slide opens in PowerPoint on your computer.

5. **Click Enable Editing on the Protected View bar near the top of your presentation window if prompted, select QST Vancouver on the title slide, then click the Drawing Tools Format tab**

QUICK TIP

Use the ScreenTips to help you find the required WordArt style.

6. **Click the More button ⊽ in the WordArt Styles group to show the selection of WordArt styles, select the WordArt style Gradient Fill - Blue-Gray, Accent 4, Reflection, then click a blank area outside the slide**

   The presentation appears in PowerPoint as shown in Figure WEB-8. Next, you save the revised version of the file to SkyDrive.

7. **Click the File tab, click Save As, notice that the path in the Address bar is to the Cengage folder on your Windows Live SkyDrive, type WEB-QST Vancouver Presentation_Revised.pptx in the File name text box, then click Save**

   The file is saved to your SkyDrive.

TROUBLE

The browser opens to the Cengage folder but the file is not visible. Follow Step 8 to open the Cengage folder and refresh thelist of files in the folder.

8. **Click the browser icon on the taskbar to open your SkyDrive page, then click Office next to your name in the SkyDrive path, view a list of recent documents, then click Cengage in the list to the left of the recent documents list to open the Cengage folder**

   Two PowerPoint files now appear in the Cengage folder.

9. **Exit the Web browser and close all tabs if prompted, then exit PowerPoint**

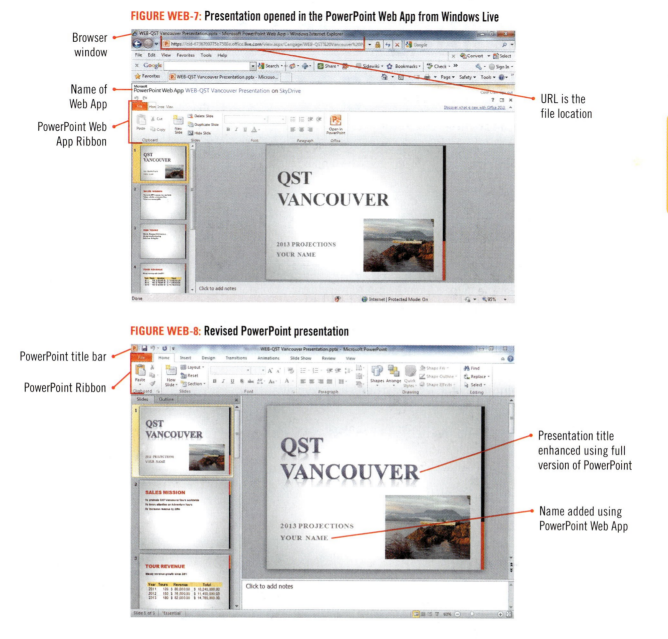

FIGURE WEB-7: Presentation opened in the PowerPoint Web App from Windows Live

Browser window

Name of Web App

PowerPoint Web App Ribbon

URL is the file location

FIGURE WEB-8: Revised PowerPoint presentation

PowerPoint title bar

PowerPoint Ribbon

Presentation title enhanced using full version of PowerPoint

Name added using PowerPoint Web App

TABLE WEB-2: Commands on the PowerPoint Web App

tab	commands available
File	• Open in PowerPoint: select to open the file in PowerPoint on your computer • Where's the Save Button?: when you click this option, a message appears telling you that you do not need to save your presentation when you are working on it with PowerPoint Web App. The presentation is saved automatically as you work. • Print • Share • Properties • Give Feedback • Privacy • Terms of Use • Close
Home	• Clipboard group: Cut, Copy, Paste • Slides group: Add a New Slide, Delete a Slide, Duplicate a Slide, and Hide a Slide • Font group: Work with text: change the font, style, color, and size of selected text • Paragraph group: Work with paragraphs: add bullets and numbers, indent text, align text • Office group: Open the file in PowerPoint on your computer
Insert	• Insert a Picture • Insert a SmartArt diagram • Insert a link such as a link to another file on SkyDrive or to a Web page
View	• Editing view (the default) • Reading view • Slide Show view • Notes view

Creating Folders and Organizing Files on SkyDrive

As you have learned, you can sign in to SkyDrive directly from the Office applications PowerPoint, Excel, Word, and OneNote, or you can access SkyDrive directly through your Web browser. This option is useful when you are away from the computer on which you normally work or when you are using a computer that does not have Office applications installed. You can go to SkyDrive, create and organize folders, and then create or open files to work on with Office Web Apps. You access SkyDrive from your Web browser, create a new folder called Illustrated, and delete one of the PowerPoint files from the My Documents folder.

STEPS

TROUBLE
Go to Step 3 if you are already signed in.

TROUBLE
Type your Windows Live ID (your e-mail) and password, then click Sign in if prompted to do so.

1. **Open your Web browser, type home.live.com in the Address bar, then press [Enter]**
   The Windows Live home page opens. From here, you can sign in to your Windows Live account and then access SkyDrive.

2. **Sign into Windows Live as directed**
   You are signed in to your Windows Live page. From this page, you can take advantage of the many applications available on Windows Live, including SkyDrive.

3. **Point to Windows Live, then click SkyDrive**
   SkyDrive opens.

4. **Click Cengage, then point to WEB-QST Vancouver Presentation.pptx**
   A menu of options for working with the file, including a Delete button to the far right, appears to the right of the filename.

5. **Click the Delete button ☒, then click OK**
   The file is removed from the Cengage folder on your SkyDrive. You still have a copy of the file on your computer.

6. **Point to Windows Live, then click SkyDrive**
   Your SkyDrive screen with the current selection of folders available on your SkyDrive opens, as shown in Figure WEB-9.

7. **Click New, click Folder, type Illustrated, click Next, click Office in the path under Add documents to Illustrated at the top of the window, then click View all in the list under Personal**
   You are returned to your list of folders, where you see the new Illustrated folder.

8. **Click Cengage, point to WEB-QST Vancouver Presentation_Revised.pptx, click More, click Move, then click the Illustrated folder**

9. **Click Move this file into Illustrated, as shown in Figure WEB-10**
   The file is moved to the Illustrated folder.

FIGURE WEB-9: Folders on your SkyDrive

Current location

Folders currently available

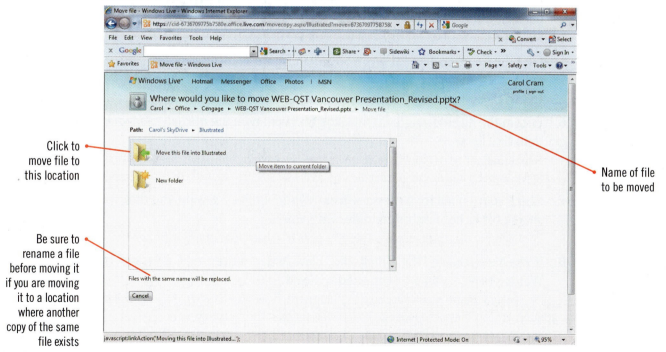

FIGURE WEB-10: Moving a file to the Illustrated folder

Click to move file to this location

Name of file to be moved

Be sure to rename a file before moving it if you are moving it to a location where another copy of the same file exists

Adding People to Your Network and Sharing Files

One of the great advantages of working with SkyDrive on Windows Live is that you can share your files with others. Suppose, for example, that you want a colleague to review a presentation you created in PowerPoint and then add a new slide. You can, of course, e-mail the presentation directly to your colleague, who can then make changes and e-mail the presentation back. Alternatively, you can save time by uploading the PowerPoint file directly to SkyDrive and then giving your colleague access to the file. Your colleague can edit the file using the PowerPoint Web App, and then you can check the updated file on SkyDrive, also using the PowerPoint Web App. In this way, you and your colleague are working with just one version of the presentation that you both can update. You have decided to share files in the Illustrated folder that you created in the previous lesson with another individual. You start by working with a partner so that you can share files with your partner and your partner can share files with you.

STEPS

TROUBLE

If you cannot find a partner, read the steps so you understand how the process works.

1. **Identify a partner with whom you can work, and obtain his or her e-mail address; you can choose someone in your class or someone on your e-mail list, but it should be someone who will be completing these steps when you are**

2. **From the Illustrated folder, click Share**

3. **Click Edit permissions**

   The Edit permissions page opens. On this page, you can select the individual with whom you would like to share the contents of the Illustrated folder.

4. **Click in the Enter a name or an e-mail address text box, type the e-mail address of your partner, then press [Tab]**

   You can define the level of access that you want to give your partner.

5. **Click the Can view files list arrow shown in Figure WEB-11, click Can add, edit details, and delete files, then click Save**

   You can choose to send a notification to each individual when you grant permission to access your files.

6. **Click in the Include your own message text box, type the message shown in Figure WEB-12, then click Send**

   Your partner will receive a message from Windows Live advising him or her that you have shared your Illustrated folder. If your partner is completing the steps at the same time, you will receive an e-mail from your partner.

TROUBLE

If you do not receive a message from Windows Live, your partner has not yet completed the steps to share the Illustrated folder.

7. **Check your e-mail for a message from Windows Live advising you that your partner has shared his or her Illustrated folder with you**

   The subject of the e-mail message will be "[Name] has shared documents with you."

QUICK TIP

You will know you are on your partner's SkyDrive because you will see your partner's first name at the beginning of the SkyDrive path.

8. **If you have received the e-mail, click View folder in the e-mail message, then sign in to Windows Live if you are requested to do so**

   You are now able to access your partner's Illustrated folder on his or her SkyDrive. You can download files in your partner's Illustrated folder to your own computer where you can work on them and then upload them again to your partner's Illustrated shared folder.

9. **Exit the browser**

FIGURE WEB-11: Editing folder permissions

Folder permissions will be changed for the Illustrated folder

Click to select network permission options

Type email address to continue to add people

Person whose permission status will change

Click to select person from list of contacts

Click to select permission option

FIGURE WEB-12: Entering a message to notify a person that file sharing permission has been granted

Sharing files on SkyDrive

When you share a folder with other people, the people with whom you share a folder can download the file to their computers and then make changes using the full version of the corresponding Office application.

Once these changes are made, each individual can then upload the file to SkyDrive and into a folder shared with you and others. In this way, you can create a network of people with whom you share your files.

Working with the Excel Web App

You can use the Excel Web App to work with an Excel spreadsheet on SkyDrive. Workbooks opened using the Excel Web App have the same look and feel as workbooks opened using the full version of Excel. However, just like the PowerPoint Web App, the Excel Web App has fewer features available than the full version of Excel. When you want to use a command that is not available on the Excel Web App, you need to open the file in the full version of Excel. You upload an Excel file containing a list of the tours offered by QST Vancouver to the Illustrated folder on SkyDrive. You use the Excel Web App to make some changes, and then you open the revised version in Excel 2010 on your computer.

STEPS

1. **Start Excel, open the file WEB-2.xlsx from the drive and folder where you store your Data Files, then save the file as WEB-QST Vancouver Tours**

   The data in the Excel file is formatted using the Excel table function.

2. **Click the File tab, click Save & Send, then click Save to Web**

   In a few moments, you should see three folders to which you can save spreadsheets. My Documents and Cengage are personal folder that contains files that only you can access. Illustrated is a shared folder that contains files you can share with others in your network. The Illustrated folder is shared with your partner.

3. **Click the Illustrated folder, click the Save As button, wait a few seconds for the Save As dialog box to appear, then click Save**

4. **Click the File tab, click Save & Send, click Save to Web, click the Windows Live SkyDrive link above your folders, then sign in if prompted**

   Windows Live opens to your SkyDrive.

5. **Click the Excel program button 🗷 on the taskbar, then exit Excel**

6. **Click your browser button on the taskbar to return to SkyDrive if SkyDrive is not the active window, click the Illustrated folder, click the Excel file, click Edit in Browser, then review the Ribbon and its tabs to familiarize yourself with the commands you can access from the Excel Web App**

   Table WEB-3 summarizes the commands that are available.

7. **Click cell A12, type Gulf Islands Sailing, press [TAB], type 3000, press [TAB], type 10, press [TAB], click cell D3, enter the formula =B3*C3, press [Enter], then click cell A1**

   The formula is copied automatically to the remaining rows as shown in Figure WEB-13 because the data in the original Excel file was created and formatted as an Excel table.

8. **Click SkyDrive in the Excel Web App path at the top of the window to return to the Illustrated folder**

   The changes you made to the Excel spreadsheet are saved automatically on SkyDrive. You can download the file directly to your computer from SkyDrive.

9. **Point to the Excel file, click More, click Download, click Save, navigate to the location where you save the files for this book, name the file WEB-QST Vancouver Tours_Updated, click Save, then click Close in the Download complete dialog box**

   The updated version of the spreadsheet is saved on your computer and on SkyDrive.

10. **Exit the Web browser**

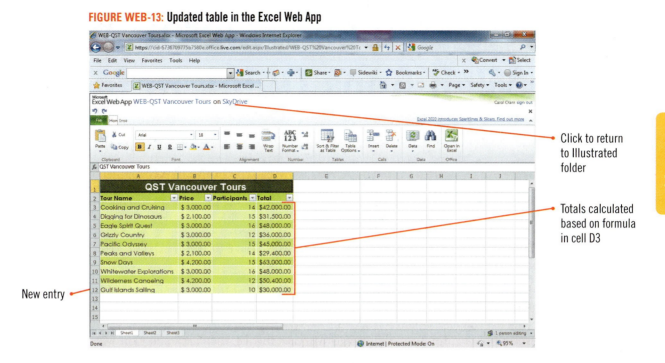

Click to return to Illustrated folder

Totals calculated based on formula in cell D3

New entry

TABLE WEB-3: Commands on the Excel Web App

tab	commands available
File	• Open in Excel: select to open the file in Excel on your computer • Where's the Save Button?: when you click this option, a message appears telling you that you do not need to save your spreadsheet when you are working in it with Excel Web App; the spreadsheet is saved automatically as you work • Save As • Share • Download a Snapshot: a snapshot contains only the values and the formatting; you cannot modify a snapshot • Download a Copy: the file can be opened and edited in the full version of Excel • Give Feedback • Privacy Statement • Terms of Use • Close
Home	• Clipboard group: Cut, Copy, Paste • Font group: change the font, style, color, and size of selected labels and values, as well as border styles and fill colors • Alignment group: change vertical and horizontal alignment and turn on the Wrap Text feature • Number group: change the number format and increase or decrease decimal places • Tables: sort and filter data in a table and modify Table Options • Cells: insert and delete cells • Data: refresh data and find labels or values • Office: open the file in Excel on your computer
Insert	• Insert a Table • Insert a Hyperlink to a Web page

Exploring other Office Web Apps

Two other Office Web Apps are Word and OneNote. You can share files on SkyDrive directly from Word or from OneNote using the same method you used to share files from PowerPoint and Excel. After you upload a Word or OneNote file to SkyDrive, you can work with it in its corresponding Office Web App. To familiarize yourself with the commands available in an Office Web App, open the file and then review the commands on each tab on the Ribbon. If you want to perform a task that is not available in the Office Web App, open the file in the full version of the application.

In addition to working with uploaded files, you can create files from new on SkyDrive. Simply sign in to SkyDrive and open a folder. With a folder open, click New and then select the Web App you want to use to create the new file.

Windows Live and Microsoft Office Web Apps Quick Reference

To Do This	Go Here
Access Windows Live	From the Web browser, type **home.live.com**, then click Sign In
Access SkyDrive on Windows Live	From the Windows Live home page, point to Windows Live, then click SkyDrive
Save to Windows Live from Word, PowerPoint, or Excel	File tab | Save & Send | Save to Web | Select a folder | Save As
Create a New Folder from Backstage view	File tab | Save & Send | Save to Web | New Folder button
Edit a File with a Web App	From SkyDrive, click the file, then click Edit in Browser
Open a File in a desktop version of the application from a Web App: Word, Excel, PowerPoint	Click Open in [Application] in the Office group in each Office Web App
Share files on Windows Live	From SkyDrive, click the folder containing the files to share, click Share on the menu bar, click Edit permissions, enter the e-mail address of the person to share files with, click the Can view files list arrow, click Can add, edit details, and delete files, then click Save

Glossary

Active The currently available document, program, or object; on the taskbar, when more than one program is open, the button for the active program appears slightly lighter.

Active cell A selected cell in an Excel worksheet.

Adjustment handle A small yellow diamond that changes the appearance of an object's most prominent feature.

Align To place objects' edges or centers on the same plane.

Animation tag Identifies the order an object is animated on a slide during a slide show.

Annotate A freehand drawing on the screen made by using the pen or highlighter tool. You can annotate only in Slide Show view.

Axis label Text in the first row and column of a worksheet that identifies data.

Background The area behind the text and graphics on a slide.

Background graphic An object placed on the slide master.

Backward-compatible Software feature that enables documents saved in an older version of a program to be opened in a newer version of the program.

Category axis The horizontal axis in a chart.

Cell The intersection of a column and row in a worksheet, datasheet, or table.

Chart A graphical representation of numerical data from a worksheet. Types include 2-D and 3-D column, bar, pie, area, and line charts.

Clip art Predesigned graphic images you can insert in any document or presentation to enhance its appearance.

Clip Organizer A library of art, pictures, sounds, video clips, and animations that all Office applications share.

Cloud computing When data, applications, and resources are stored on servers accessed over the Internet or a company's internal network rather than on user's computers.

Collections The folders in the Clip Organizer where the clip art is stored.

Column heading The gray box containing the column letter on top of the columns in the worksheet.

Content placeholder A placeholder that is used to enter text or objects such as clip art, charts, or pictures.

Compatibility The ability of different programs to work together and exchange data.

Crop To hide part of an object, such as clip art using the Cropping tool or to delete a part of a picture.

Data series A column or row in a datasheet.

Data series marker A graphical representation of a data series, such as a bar or column.

Digital signature A way to authenticate a presentation files using computer cryptography. A digital signature is not visible in a presentation.

Distribute To evenly divide the space horizontally or vertically between objects relative to each other or the slide edges.

Document Inspector A PowerPoint feature that examines a presentation for hidden data or personal information.

Embedded object An object that is created in one application and inserted to another. Embedded objects remain connected to the original program file in which they were created for editing.

Exception A change you make directly to text on the slide, which does not match the theme fonts on the slide master.

Gallery A visual collection of choices you can browse through to make a selection. Often available with Live Preview.

Group To combine multiple objects into one object.

Insertion point A blinking vertical line that indicates where the next character will appear when text is entered in a text placeholder in PowerPoint.

Integrate To incorporate a document and parts of a document created in one program into another program; for example, to incorporate an Excel chart into a PowerPoint slide, or an Access table into a Word document.

Interface The look and feel of a program; for example, the appearance of commands and the way they are organized in the program window.

Launch To open or start a program on your computer.

Legend Text that provides information about the data series in a chart.

Live Preview A feature that shows you the result of an action such as a theme change before you apply the change.

Masters One of three views that stores information about the presentation theme, fonts, placeholders, and other background objects. The three views are Slide Master view, Handout Master view, and Notes Master view.

Metadata Another name for document properties that includes the author name, the document subject, the document title, and other personal information.

Microsoft Graph A program that creates a chart to graphically depict numerical information when you don't have access to Microsoft Excel.

Mini toolbar A small toolbar that appears next to selected text that contains basic text-formatting commands.

Normal view The primary view that you use to write, edit, and design your presentation. Normal view is divided into three areas: Slides or Outline tab, Slide pane, and Notes pane.

Notes Page view A presentation view that displays a reduced image of the current slide above a large text box where you can type notes.

Notes pane The area in Normal view that shows speaker notes for the current slide; also in Notes Page view, the area below the slide image that contains speaker notes.

Object An item you place or draw on a slide that can be modified. Examples of objects include drawn lines and shapes, text, clip art, and imported pictures.

Office Web App Versions of the Microsoft Office applications with limited functionality that are available online from Windows Live SkyDrive. Users can view documents online and then edit them in the browser using a selection of functions. Office Web Apps are available for Word, PowerPoint, Excel, and One Note.

Online collaboration The ability to incorporate feedback or share information across the Internet or a company network or intranet.

Outline tab The section in Normal view that displays your presentation text in the form of an outline, without graphics.

Pane A section of the PowerPoint window, such as the Slide or Notes pane.

Picture A digital photograph, piece of line art, or clip art that is created in another program and is inserted into PowerPoint.

PowerPoint Viewer A special application designed to run a PowerPoint slide show on any compatible computer that does not have PowerPoint installed.

PowerPoint window A window that contains the running PowerPoint application. The PowerPoint window includes the Ribbon, panes, and Presentation window.

Presentation software A software program used to organize and present information.

Previewing Prior to printing, seeing onscreen exactly how the printed document will look.

Quick Access toolbar A small toolbar on the left side of a Microsoft application program window's title bar, containing icons that you click to quickly perform common actions, such as saving a file.

Quick Style Determines how fonts, colors, and effects of the theme are combined and which color, font, and effect is dominant. A Quick Style can be applied to shapes or text.

Reading view A view you use to review your presentation or present a slide show to someone on a computer monitor.

Read-only A file that can't be edited or modified.

Ribbon A wide (toolbar-like) band that runs across the PowerPoint window that organizes primary commands into tabs; each tab has buttons organized into groups.

Rotate handle A green circular handle at the top of a selected object that you can drag to rotate the selected object.

Row heading The gray box containing the row number to the left of the row in a worksheet.

Scale To change the size of a graphic to a specific percentage of its original size.

Screen capture An electronic snapshot of your screen, as if you took a picture of it with a camera, which you can paste into a document.

Selection box A dashed border that appears around a text object or placeholder, indicating that it is ready to accept text.

Series in Columns The data in the datasheet columns is plotted on the y-axis, and the row axis labels are shown in the legend. The column axis labels are plotted on the x-axis.

Series in Rows The data in the datasheet rows is plotted on the y-axis, and the row axis labels are shown on the x-axis.

Sizing handles The small circles and squares that appear around a selected object. Dragging a sizing handle resizes the object.

SkyDrive An online storage and file sharing service. Access to SkyDrive is through a Windows Live account. Up to 25 GB of data can be stored in a personal SkyDrive, with each file a maximum size of 50 MB.

Slide layout This determines how all of the elements on a slide are arranged, including text and content placeholders.

Slide pane The section of Normal view that contains the current slide.

Slide Show view A view that shows a presentation as an electronic slide show; each slide fills the screen.

Slide Sorter view A view that displays a thumbnail of all slides in the order in which they appear in your presentation; used to rearrange slides and slide transitions.

Slide timing The amount of time a slide is visible on the screen during a slide show.

Slide transition The special effect that moves one slide off the screen and the next slide on the screen during a slide show. Each slide can have its own transition effect.

Slides tab The section in Normal view that displays the slides of your presentation as small thumbnails.

SmartArt A professional quality graphic diagram that visually illustrates text.

SmartArt Style A pre-set combination of formatting options that follows the design theme that you can apply to a SmartArt graphic.

Status bar The bar at the bottom of the PowerPoint window that contains messages about what you are doing and seeing in PowerPoint, such as the current slide number or the current theme.

Subtitle text placeholder A box on the title slide reserved for subpoint text.

Suite A group of programs that are bundled together and share a similar interface, making it easy to transfer skills and program content among them.

Tab A section of the Ribbon that identifies groups of commands like the Home tab.

Task pane A separate pane that contains sets of menus, lists, options, and hyperlinks such as the Animation task pane that are used to customize objects.

Template A type of presentation that contains custom design information made to the slide master, slide layouts, and theme.

Text label A text box you create using the Text Box button, where the text does not automatically wrap inside the box. Text box text does not appear in the Outline tab.

Text placeholder A box with a dotted border and text that you replace with your own text.

Theme A set of colors, fonts, and effects that you apply to a presentation from the Themes Gallery.

Theme colors The set of 12 coordinated colors that make up a PowerPoint presentation; a color scheme assigns colors for text, lines, fills, accents, hyperlinks, and background.

Theme effects The set of effects for lines and fills.

Theme fonts The set of fonts for titles and other text.

Thumbnail A small image of a slide. Thumbnails are visible on the Slides tab and in Slide Sorter view.

Title The first line or heading on a slide.

Title placeholder A box on a slide reserved for the title of a presentation or slide.

Title slide The first slide in a presentation.

User interface A collective term for all the ways you interact with a software program.

Value axis The vertical axis in a chart.

View A way of displaying a presentation, such as Normal view, Reading view, Notes Page view, Slide Sorter view, and Slide Show view.

View Shortcuts The buttons at the bottom of the PowerPoint window on the status bar that you click to switch among views.

Windows Live A collection of services and Web applications that people can access through a login. Windows Live services include access to e-mail and instant messaging, storage of files on SkyDrive, sharing and storage of photos, networking with people, downloading software, and interfacing with a mobile device.

Word processing box A text box you create using the Text Box button, where the text automatically wraps inside the box.

WordArt A set of decorative styles or text effects that is applied to text.

Worksheet Where the numerical data is stored for a chart.

XML Acronym that stands for eXtensible Markup Language, which is a language used to structure, store, and send information.

Zooming in A feature that makes a document appear larger but shows less of it on screen at once; does not affect actual document size.

Zooming out A feature that shows more of a document on screen at once but at a reduced size; does not affect actual document size.

Zoom slider A feature that allows you to change the zoom percentage of a slide. Located in the status bar.

Index